# Radicalizing Rawls

# PHILOSOPHY, PUBLIC POLICY, AND TRANSNATIONAL LAW

*Series Editor: John Martin Gillroy, Professor of International Relations and Founding Director of the Graduate Programs in Environmental Policy Design at Lehigh University. http://ir.cas2.lehigh.edu/content/john-martin-gillroy*

**A Note from the Editor:**
This new series for Palgrave-Macmillan seeks, for the first time at a major publisher, to take the philosophical and public policy foundations of legal practice seriously, that is, not in terms of bits and pieces of theory or policy used to illustrate empirical claims, but as a systematic and integral basis for the study of codified law. The series will pursue scholarship that integrates the superstructure of the positive law with its philosophical and public policy substructure producing a more three-dimensional understanding of transnational law and its evolution, meaning, imperatives and future.

For the purposes of this series, transnational law includes the traditional categories of comparative and international law and seeks to understand the role of, not just states, but persons, international organizations, NGOs and governments that create or use law that transcends sovereign states. The series encourages an interdisciplinary approach to transnational law and seeks research reports, original manuscripts or edited collections that explore the essence of legal practice in both the public policy arguments that inform legal discourse and the philosophical precepts that create the logic of concepts inherent in policy debate. The series aims to expand the types and use of philosophical and policy paradigms exploring the nature of transnational law, so that its empirical dimensions are better illuminated for practitioners and scholars alike.

*An Evolutionary Paradigm for International Law: Philosophical Method, David Hume, and the Essence of Sovereignty*
By John Martin Gillroy

*Radicalizing Rawls: Global Justice and the Foundations of International Law*
By Gary Chartier

# Radicalizing Rawls
*Global Justice and the Foundations of International Law*

Gary Chartier

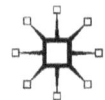

RADICALIZING RAWLS
Copyright © Gary Chartier, 2014.
Softcover reprint of the hardcover 1st edition 2014 978-1-137-38290-0
All rights reserved.

First published in 2014 by PALGRAVE MACMILLAN® in the United States—a division of St. Martin's Press LLC, 175 Fifth Avenue, New York, NY 10010.

Where this book is distributed in the UK, Europe and the rest of the world, this is by Palgrave Macmillan, a division of Macmillan Publishers Limited, registered in England, company number 785998, of Houndmills, Basingstoke, Hampshire RG21 6XS.

Palgrave Macmillan is the global academic imprint of the above companies and has companies and representatives throughout the world.

Palgrave® and Macmillan® are registered trademarks in the United States, the United Kingdom, Europe and other countries.

ISBN 978-1-349-48026-5     ISBN 978-1-137-38297-9 (eBook)
DOI 10.1057/9781137382979
Library of Congress Cataloging-in-Publication Data

Chartier, Gary, author.
  Radicalizing Rawls : global justice and the foundations of international law / Gary Chartier.
      pages cm
  Includes bibliographical references and index.

  1. Rawls, John, 1921–2002. Law of peoples. 2. International law—Philosophy. 3. Human rights. 4. Liberalism. 5. Social justice. 6. Social contract. I. Title.

KZ1256.C47 2014
341.01—dc23                                              2013033455

A catalogue record of the book is available from the British Library.

Design by Scribe Inc.

First edition: February 2014

10 9 8 7 6 5 4 3 2 1

*For Drid, with all my love*

# Contents

| | | |
|---|---|---|
| Acknowledgments | | ix |
| Introduction | | 1 |
| 1 | Rawls's Starting Point | 5 |
| 2 | Rawls's Explicit Defense of the Equality of Peoples | 13 |
| 3 | Challenging the Global Primacy of Peoples | 27 |
| 4 | Defining and Implementing a Law of Persons | 81 |
| 5 | Market Democracy, Market Anarchy, and Global Justice | 121 |
| Conclusion | | 151 |
| Notes | | 157 |
| About the Author | | 189 |
| Index | | 191 |

# Acknowledgments

I owe multiple debts of gratitude in connection with *Radicalizing Rawls*. In particular, I want to thank

- Elenor Webb for welcome opportunities for dialogue and for ongoing moral support, as also for her persistent playfulness, sense of wonder, and love;
- Lee Wilson, for nearly three decades of warm and supportive friendship;
- Carole Pateman, Seana Shiffrin, Thomas W. Pogge, Richard Steinberg, Charles Beitz, David Gordon, Ponnekanti Samata Chari, and multiple anonymous readers for reading and reacting to the manuscript;
- Barbara Herman, Annette Bryson, Roger E. Rustad Jr., and Linn Marie Tonstad for their willingness to review it;
- Fernando R. Tesón, Patrick Hayden, Kok-Chor Tan, and John Tomasi for their willingness to endorse the book;
- Elyn Saks, Ronald Garet, Michael Shapiro, and Scott Altman for a useful conversation about Rawls and the Law of Peoples;
- Thomas Ayres, Lindsey Barrett, Ben Dunlap, and Maria Isabel Guerrero for editorial assistance;
- Thomas W. Pogge and Fernando R. Tesón for supplying copies of relevant essays;
- Deborah K. Dunn for valuable exchanges during the time my earliest work on Rawls was being written and edited;
- David Schmidtz, John Tomasi, Steve Munzer, and John Finnis for inspiring insight and reflection;
- Brian O'Connor, for his consistent and enthusiastic support for the book;

x • Acknowledgments

- Scarlet Neath, for her assistance with the project at numerous points;
- Daniel King, for copy-editing the manuscript and making my prose more readable;
- the team at AntiWar.com (to which my author royalties for this book will be donated) for its persistent support for peace and opposition to militarism and imperialism;
- journal editors for reprint permissions;[1]
- my comrades at the Center for a Stateless Society—including Sheldon Richman, Kevin Carson, Charles W. Johnson, Roderick T. Long, Anthony Gregory, Brad Spangler, Chris Lempa, Joseph Stromberg, James Tuttle, Roman Pearah, Anna O. Morgenstern, Tom Knapp, Darian Worden, David S. D'Amato, Tennyson McCalla, Mike Gogulski, Christiaan Elderhorst, Dawie Coetzee, Ross Kenyon, Trevor Hultner, Natasha Petrova, Less Antman, Mariana Evica, Stephanie Murphy, Wendy McElroy, Jason Lee Byas, Alan Furth, Stephan Kinsella, William Gillis, Dave Hummels, George van der Meer, Julia Riber Pitt, and Jeremy Weiland—for analysis, activism, and friendship; *and*
- the usual suspects—Elenor Webb, Jeffrey Cassidy, Annette Bryson, Aena Prakash, Alexander Lian, Andrew Howe, Angela Keaton, Anne-Marie Pearson, Bart Willruth, Carole Pateman, Charles W. Teel Jr., Chelsea Krafve, Craig R. Kinzer, David B. Hoppe, David Gordon, David R. Larson, Deborah K. Dunn, Donna Carlson, Ellen Hubbell, Eva Pascal, Fritz Guy, Heather Ferguson, Jan M. Holden, Jesse Leamon, Joel Sandefur, John Elder, John Thomas, Julio C. Muñoz, Kenneth A. Dickey, Lawrence T. Geraty, Less Antman, Ligia Radoias, Maria Zlateva, Michael Orlando, Nabil Abu-Assal, Pamela J. Stubbart, Patricia M. Cabrera, Robert E. Rustad Jr., Ronel Harvey, Ruth E. E. Burke, Sarvi Sheybany, Sel J. Hwahng, Sheldon Richman, W. Kent Rogers, and Wonil Kim—for the usual things.

John Rawls died while I was completing what turns out in retrospect to have been the first draft of this book. I am not a Rawlsian;[2] but I believe Rawls's work deserves careful attention because of the importance of the issues he addresses, the care with which he tackles them, and the enormous influence his approach has exerted and continues to exert. I hope this book helps advance the conversation his work has initiated and serves as a modest tribute to his vast contributions to contemporary Anglo-American moral, political, and legal theory.

# Introduction

An attractively Rawlsian account of justice and the normative grounds of law across our planet should be cosmopolitan in its motivation and foundations; it should be understood as consonant with the rejection of the Westphalian state and as providing a framework within which that rejection might be justified. While it would differ from Rawls's own account of global justice, it could qualify as Rawlsian because it would seek to extend Rawls's understanding of domestic justice, suitably modified, to the global level and because it could be grounded in a Rawlsian account of the justification of societal institutions.

Rawls's *The Law of Peoples* articulates a set of proposed norms for global justice, international law, and the foreign policy of a reasonably just liberal state (or, as Rawls prefers, "people"). These norms are grounded in an original position (or, more precisely, two parallel original positions) structurally similar to the one he famously employs in framing principles of domestic justice. But the deliberators at the global level are understood to represent peoples rather than individuals. Rawls envisions the Law of Peoples these deliberators would endorse as acceptable to both liberals and those he calls "decent" nonliberals (Chapter 1).

Rawls's defense of his decision to treat peoples rather than persons as foundational at the global level is surprisingly thin (Chapter 2). There are multiple rationales Rawls might have offered or that other Rawlsians might offer for this decision to opt for a people-based rather than a cosmopolitan starting point. Some of these rationales seem unconvincing. And a cosmopolitan could argue convincingly for a range of modifications to Rawls's assumptions and approach that would render the others ineffective as responses to cosmopolitanism. Ultimately, a cosmopolitan starting point for reflection on the problem of global justice seems preferable to a people-based approach, and the terms of justice at the global level should be seen as foundational—setting the bounds for any more local formulations (Chapter 3).

While its content would overlap with that of a Rawlsian Law of Peoples, a cosmopolitan Law of Persons would feature more robust human rights norms than Rawls's people-based approach; its core contents would be the Rawlsian equal basic liberties, plus additional safeguards for productive property and freedom of global movement (John Tomasi's proposals regarding the shape of Rawlsian domestic justice could prove helpful here, though they probably merit expansion). A Law of Persons would also contain requirements likely to be more protective of individuals in wartime than Rawls's people-based account. There might well be good reason for the governments of liberal peoples to avoid the use of military force or sanctions to compel decent nonliberals to adopt liberal policies. A Law of Persons would, however, permit a variety of other responses to decent nonliberals' violations of what liberals would take to be defensible human right (Chapter 4).

Some readers of Rawls who adopt the cosmopolitan position I do here might suggest that Rawls ought to be committed to embracing a social-democratic global state. In fact, however, a suitably corrected Rawlsian account of global justice may be seen as consonant with a rejection not only of such a global government but, indeed, of the Westphalian state as well. Rawlsian domestic justice can be recast in a more market-friendly way in something like the manner suggested by Tomasi.[1] If cosmopolitan global justice is to be understood as taking the same form as Rawlsian domestic justice, then reasons to rethink domestic justice along what Tomasi calls market-democratic lines would apply at the global level as well. But it might be possible to radicalize Tomasi's position—to show that market anarchy, domestically and globally, could be seen as an attractive species of market democracy. The viability of a global order lacking the oversight of a world state, acknowledged by many cosmopolitan Rawlsians, points to the potential viability of such a project, which could include a viable conception of global distributive justice (Chapter 5).

A Law of Persons—a recognizably Rawlsian account of global justice rooted in a cosmopolitan starting point—appears attractive and credible. Such an account could feature extensive human rights protections, requirements of global distributive justice, and constraints on armed conflict. Cosmopolitans not committed to the creation of a world state already agree that order can be maintained without the activity of a territorial monopolist and that distributive justice can be conceived of coherently and appealingly without the operation of such a monopolist as a distributor. So they might have reason to agree that, if market democracy proved defensible, global market anarchy could prove defensible as well, and so to support a global Law of Persons safeguarding an anarchic variety of market democracy (Conclusion).

My goal here is not to provide definitive answers to questions about what Rawls's own views were or should, on his own assumptions, have been—this is not a work of biography or textual interpretation—but rather to explore a direction in which a Rawlsian position, attentive to Rawls's texts but not constrained by all his substantive or methodological commitments, might develop. But my focus throughout *is* on Rawls's own texts, particularly *The Law of Peoples* and *A Theory of Justice* (where Rawls first sketched a version of his Law of Peoples). I certainly seek to be attentive to defenses of his position offered by various contemporary Rawlsians. But my goal is to understand and critique Rawls's own position as he explicitly articulated it and to build on that position as I elaborate an alternative in continuity with, though obviously different in important ways from, that position. In doing so, I am not attempting to claim that Rawls was, deep down, a cosmopolitan, but rather that a cosmopolitanism that extends (a suitably modified version of) Rawls's account of domestic justice to the global level is preferable to Rawls's own people-focused account while still reflective in important ways of his own perspective. Intended to be Rawlsian in virtue of its general method and justificatory approach, as well as the spirit of many of its substantive conclusions, *Radicalizing Rawls* engages with Rawls's texts as enormously influential examples of contemporary anticosmopolitanism while seeking to move beyond them toward a more plausible, still broadly Rawlsian, account of global justice.

# CHAPTER 1

# Rawls's Starting Point

## I. Rawls's Understanding of Global Justice Is People Based

Rawls offers an account of global justice and the grounds of global law expressed in what he calls "the Law of Peoples."[1] Peoples are like states, but they lack some of the more obviously dubious features of states (Part II). It is representatives of peoples whose deliberation in a (two-part) global version of Rawls's familiar "original position" yields the content of the Law of Peoples; thus, Rawls's approach treats peoples as basic to a just global order (Part III). Such a Law would contain what Rawls takes to be the most crucial elements of a refined version of current international law (Part IV). The broad category of "well-ordered" peoples includes both liberal peoples and those Rawls calls "decent nonliberal" peoples (Part V). Rawls's adoption of a people-based approach leads to conclusions that are less appealing from the standpoint of individuals around the globe than a cosmopolitan alternative (Part VI). His entire project, organized around the needs and concerns of peoples, reflects the features of his starting point (Part VII).

## II. Peoples Exhibit Many, but Not All, of the Features of States

Rawls treats peoples as the foundational elements of the global order elaborated in the Law of Peoples.

He attends to two kinds of peoples: *liberal peoples* and *decent nonliberal peoples*—these two groups together constituting a group he terms *well-ordered peoples*. His theory also address three other kinds of political units: *outlaw states, societies burdened by unfavorable conditions,* and *benevolent absolutisms.*[2]

United by its members' "common sympathies,"[3] a *people* is not a *state*. A state, for Rawls, is an entity that claims to be sovereign; peoples, by contrast, are organized societies that lack the kind of *absolute* sovereignty characteristically predicated of Westphalian states.[4] Thus, peoples do not suppose themselves free to use military force—except to defend themselves or others against aggression—or to abuse the globally recognized human rights of persons within their borders.[5] In addition, according to Rawls, peoples differ from states because states are primarily or exclusively self-interested.[6] The interests, and therefore the actions, of states are unlimited by justice.[7] By contrast, we can, Rawls supposes, attribute moral motives to peoples.[8]

The rights and duties of peoples are rooted in the Law of Peoples, which can be understood as a product of their own reasonable agreement.[9] Peoples, Rawls imagines, treat other peoples as their equals[10] and accept reasonable limits on their behavior,[11] acknowledging and acting on principle rather than focusing exclusively on the satisfaction of their own interests by whatever means prove necessary.[12]

Peoples might be expected to be structured on the basis of cultural affinity. But Rawls does not imply that peoples will or should be constructed from scratch. Rather, we may assume that peoples will typically be transformed versions of existing states—ones whose domestic political institutions and attitudes toward other societies take on appropriate characteristics.[13]

## III. Peoples Play Foundational Roles in Rawls's Second Original Position

The Law of Peoples is understood as the product of (two-part) deliberation in a global original position.

*A Theory of Justice* introduced Rawls's readers to an imaginative device that embodies some of our culture's most deeply rooted convictions about justice. We should think of a society's legal-cum-political rules and institutions as fair, he suggests, if they conform to principles that representatives of the society's members would adopt behind a "veil of ignorance" in the "original position."[14] This device is best seen as a way of dramatizing what it would mean for people to choose reasonably—the focus is not on, say, how people with particular psychic characteristics likely *would* choose but on how reasonable people *should* choose.[15]

People deliberating behind a domestic veil of ignorance do not know the circumstances, abilities, life chances, or moral or religious convictions of those they represent in the real world of their society.[16] Thus, the deliberators in the original position, all of whom are equal in status and influence, would settle on the requirement that everyone enjoy "the same indefeasible claim to a fully adequate scheme of equal basic liberties, which scheme is compatible with the same scheme of liberties for all."[17] For Rawls, the basic liberties enjoy "lexical priority": they cannot be infringed in the interests of material well-being (though Rawls sometimes seems to have doubts about this). Deliberators in the original position would judge social and economic inequalities appropriate only if "attached to offices and positions open to all under conditions of fair equality of opportunity."[18] And they would likely decide that institutions shaping the distribution of wealth in their society should be shaped in accordance with what Rawls terms the "Difference Principle," according to which basic legal and political rules and institutions should be structured in such a way that they work to the advantage—indeed, that they maximize the welfare—of the class made up of those who are least well off—the working poor.[19]

Rawls envisions another sort of original position, this time global, in *The Law of Peoples*. While the occupants of the original position at the domestic level represent individuals or families,[20] the "second original position" at the global level is occupied by representatives of *peoples*, viewed as unitary entities.[21] Deliberation in the original position at the global level takes place in two phases. In the first, only liberal societies are represented. The principles of global justice endorsed in this original position are then shown to be acceptable to decent nonliberal peoples represented in a second original position in which liberal societies do not participate. There is no global original position within which *both* liberal and nonliberal societies participate simultaneously. It will be simpler, however, to refer subsequently to Rawls's account of global justice as involving "a global original position."[22]

### IV. Rawls's Law of Peoples Features a Version of Contemporary International Law Norms

Rawls's Law of Peoples comprises a set of norms designed to guide the "*foreign policy* of a reasonably just *liberal* people,"[23] though these norms are also ultimately intended to structure the "realistic utopia" Rawls calls "the Society of Peoples"—a cooperative, peaceful, global community.[24] The Law of Peoples is intended to be followed by individual societies—whether or not those societies or others are committed to its principles. Thus, even in a world in which many peoples did not conform to this Law, individual peoples would still be bound by it and could rightly demand that others conform to it.[25]

A just Law of Peoples, for Rawls, is one that would be endorsed behind a veil of ignorance among representatives of (the dominant actors in) both liberal and decent nonliberal societies. The Law of Peoples is a refinement of current norms of international law.[26] Rawlsian deliberators do not reflect (like their counterparts at the domestic level) on a potentially unlimited range of possible conceptions of justice. Instead, they are depicted as beginning with, and evaluating, existing international law norms and as going on to embrace principles safeguarding their independence and equality of status, requiring them to keep their agreements, limiting their forcible intervention in one another's affairs, protecting their rights to self-defense, limiting their rights to go to war to defensive cases, requiring justice in war and respect for human rights, holding them responsible for agreements made in their names or on their behalf, and requiring assistance for burdened societies.[27] Rawls suggests that equal representatives of well-ordered peoples, deliberating behind a veil of ignorance, would endorse these traditional principles with some qualifications,[28] with the addition of rules related to the operation of associations of particular peoples, to trade, and to other common activities.[29]

### V. Decent Nonliberals Respect Some, but Not All, Human Rights

A nonliberal society qualifies as *decent*, in Rawls's terms, if it meets several conditions.

- It must not be aggressive. Its legal order must serve the common good and protect human rights.
- Its legal norms must possess moral legitimacy from the standpoint of its people. It must view its people as responsible moral actors.
- Its officials must act on the assumption that its legal and political order does and must embody a genuine concern for the common good.[30]

While he observes that other models are possible, Rawls focuses on (imagined) decent hierarchical peoples he depicts as *associationist* as examples of decent nonliberal peoples.[31] In these societies, people are related to the body politic as members of various societal groups with presumed commonalities of interest. An associationist model, Rawls suggests, might be preferred by those who find liberal society deracinated and who conceive of individuals' identities as to a great degree conferred by the groups to which they belong.[32] A decent hierarchical society seeks and preserves the common good by means of an array of bodies representing various organic social groups, all of which must be consulted before important public decisions are made,[33] with the understanding that every member of a decent hierarchical society is a member of one or more represented groups.[34] Because each group's views must be taken into account by policy makers, membership in the various represented groups offers opportunities for people to express opinions regarding matters of public concern and to challenge government positions, and government officials are required to respond to challenges,[35] justifying their policies with reference to the common good,[36] making clear how their policies sustain a fair cooperative social scheme.[37]

Rawls evidently opts for this consultative structure because there is, he suggests, some historical precedent for it in Muslim political theory.[38] He proposes an imagined Muslim people, Kazanistan, as a model decent nonliberal society, perhaps because he is concerned with the viability for Muslims in particular of the consultative hierarchical model he has proposed.[39]

A decent nonliberal society may have an official religion—or an official comprehensive doctrine of some other kind. That it does, however, need not call into question its status as a decent society, because it declines to propagate its comprehensive doctrine by force and it allows those who do not share it to practice their traditions without fear.[40] It may, however, privilege adherents of the dominant comprehensive doctrine by, for instance, giving them the exclusive right to hold certain major public offices.[41]

Representatives of (the dominant actors within) decent hierarchical peoples,[42] Rawls is confident, would endorse the Law of Peoples in the original position.[43] This means both that liberals could reasonably expect them to adhere to the Law of Peoples and that they deserve to be tolerated by liberal societies. Thus, while the stance toward religious plurality Rawls has attributed to an imagined associationist society is not—like other features of such a society's public order—"fully reasonable," it *is* compatible with the society's being *decent* and so with its meriting tolerance from liberal societies.[44]

## VI. A Cosmopolitan Alternative Would Give Individuals, Rather Than Peoples, Pride of Place

"The original sin that continues to haunt the state and the international system . . . [is that] these are artificial entities created and maintained to perpetuate the Westphalian balance of power."[45] But Rawls's account of the normative grounds of global law seems, with relatively minor modifications, to presuppose the existence and legitimacy of these artificial entities. That it does—particularly given that both liberal and decent nonliberal peoples must approve the Law of Peoples—has negative implications for individual persons as regards human rights, economic issues, and the conduct of war.

By Rawls's own admission, his Law of Peoples is rooted in "an original position at the second level that is fair to peoples and not to individual persons."[46] His Law treats individual persons unequally in at least two ways. By treating vastly different peoples equally, it treats the members of these peoples unequally, because a given person's interests will count for more or less depending on the size, status, culture, and wealth of the people of which she is a member. And by treating each people as a unitary entity, it denies equal consideration to the interests and perspectives of some members of every people and runs the risk of effectively ignoring the interests and perspectives of dissenters and outsiders.[47] A Rawlsian Law of Peoples also seems effectively to bracket questions about the appropriateness of any given people's claim to jurisdiction over the territory it claims (even if, as I would deny, there might in principle be justifiable claims by territorially monopolistic states to control "their" territory).[48] And it makes it easier for a society's rulers to disregard the interests of outsiders, particularly in wartime.

A cosmopolitan equivalent to the Law of Peoples, a Law of Persons, by contrast, would treat the interests of particular persons as equal and distinguishable. Such a Law, formulated by deliberators representing persons rather than peoples, might be expected to embody a global version of whatever account of domestic justice can be defended along Rawlsian lines.[49] Featuring consistent rights for particular persons and generally applicable principles of justice, it would necessarily constrain choices about institutions at the local level. Applying to all individuals without regard to their circumstances, it would presumably limit the arrangements it would be reasonable to support at the local level.

## VII. Rawls's Law of Peoples Is People Based, with Problematic Consequences for Persons

Rawls frames normative grounds for global law using a global original position in which peoples, rather than persons, are represented equally. Peoples aren't identical with states—they lack a few of states' worst features—but they are still territorial monopolists, and it is primarily to them that persons are expected, on Rawls's view, to look for justice. While it is not unreasonable to call the Law of Peoples an account of global justice—since it protects certain rights—like Rawls's first principle of domestic justice, the primary site of justice for Rawls is the people.

Rawls's Law of Peoples is hardly radical, comprising, as it does, norms largely familiar from existing international law. Unsurprisingly, given that it must be generated in a way likely to find acceptance among decent nonliberal peoples, it treats the laws and other institutions of such peoples with respect. But it is because Rawls's Law treats *peoples* of any sort, liberal or decent nonliberal, as foundational that it can't be expected to take the interests of individuals with sufficient seriousness and why it might "seem to accept global apartheid."[50]

Rawls's people-based starting point receives surprisingly thin argumentative support in *The Law of Peoples*. In Chapter 2, I explain how he attempts to warrant his position, and why his explicit arguments seem unpersuasive.

# CHAPTER 2

# Rawls's Explicit Defense of the Equality of Peoples

## I. What Rawls Says in Support of Treating Equal Peoples, Rather Than Equal Persons, as Globally Foundational Doesn't Seem Persuasive

Rawls's explicit arguments in the text of *The Law of Peoples* for the equality of peoples, and against the equality of persons, at the global level are surprisingly thin. His account of domestic justice incorporates what people might take to be plausible reasons for recognizing one another as morally and politically equal (Part II). But he rather quickly dismisses the idea of using an original position in which persons are treated equally in order to formulate requirements at the global level (Part III). And the positive arguments he advances for the equality of peoples are relatively insubstantial (Part IV). Better arguments than Rawls's own are needed to defend a people-based to a person-based starting point for reflection on justice at the global level on Rawlsian grounds (Part V).

## II. Rawls Defends the Equality of Persons at the Domestic Level in Light of Generic Characteristics

The considerations that lead Rawls to opt for an original position populated by individual deliberators at the domestic level might seem to apply with equal force when the second original position is being designed.[1] In the course of elaborating his account of domestic justice, he writes that it makes sense "to suppose that the parties in the original position are equal. That is, all have the same rights in the procedure for choosing principles; each can make proposals, submit reasons for their acceptance, and so on. Obviously the purpose of these conditions is to represent equality between human beings as moral persons, as creatures having a conception of their good and capable of a sense of justice. The basis of equality is taken to be similarity in these two respects."[2]

In *A Theory of Justice*, the capacity to engage in shared reflection on the norms governing political life seems to be the key condition for equality in the original position. "[E]qual justice is owed to those who have the capacity to take part in and to act in accordance with the public understanding of the initial situation."[3] Those deliberating in the domestic original position—and, by implication, those they represent—are equal in that each has certain minimum capacities required for pursuing personal goals and assessing the fairness of social arrangements.

Like other aspects of justice as fairness, the moral and political equality of persons can and must be validated through a process of deliberation leading, ultimately, to wide reflective equilibrium among the deliberators' relevant moral and political beliefs.[4] But Rawls's defense is framed in general terms that do not obviously depend on substantial background assumptions about persons or political life and that don't seem rooted in any thick tradition of moral or political discourse.[5]

His focus here is on the participants in a single, closed society. He does not need, for much of his argument in *A Theory of Justice*, to reach the question whether the kind of equality with which he is concerned is equality simply among members of that society. However, his discussion of justice in war toward the end of the book implies that he believes that requirements binding across societies can be seen as grounded in the same kind of normative reasoning that underlies his account of domestic justice. And a natural way to read this is to conclude that, if pressed, he would have acknowledged that there was an important sense in which people across state or societal boundaries should, on his view, treat one another as equals, even if not everyone would have been entitled to equal consideration in the determination of principles of justice *for a given state*.[6] Given Rawls's goal of embracing contractualism all the way down, it seems, indeed, as if the most obvious way to justify moral principles constraining the treatment of persons across societies would be to see the requirements governing such treatment to emerge from a global contracting procedure.

## III. Rawls's Rejection of the Equality of Persons at the Global Level Is Undeveloped

Rawls explicitly rejects the idea of a global original position featuring individual deliberators as the basis for the Law of Peoples.[7] We should not attempt, he says, to derive a set of global norms by imagining all individual persons around the world as deliberating in the original position. Advocating a cosmopolitan approach "amounts to saying that all persons are to have the equal liberal rights of citizens in a constitutional democracy."[8] And we could know that they should, that putatively decent nonliberal societies don't pass moral muster, only in view of "a reasonable liberal Law of Peoples."[9] The fact that we can envision "a [cosmopolitan] global original position" doesn't demonstrate that a liberal account of global justice is the only reasonable option, "and we can't merely assume it."[10]

However, the procedure Rawls proposes for the derivation of the Law of Peoples seems designed to guarantee precisely, among other things, that decent nonliberal peoples *are* viewed as acceptable, so it's hard to see the Law of Peoples as settling the question whether persons ought to be viewed as equal at the global level.[11] He emphasizes that those deliberating at the global level "are the representatives of equal peoples, and equal peoples will want to maintain this equality with each other."[12] Thus, the rejection of cosmopolitanism is as much a consequence of the structure of the second original position as the rejection of hierarchy is of the structure of the first.[13]

But the original position is designed to represent "what we would regard—you and I, here and now—as fair conditions under which the parties . . . are to specify the Law of Peoples."[14] Why do we have good reason to treat peoples as equal? Rawls *specifies* equality among the parties.[15] He may be right that symmetry is fair here. But he hasn't *shown* that it is simply by asserting that it is.

Persons are equal in the first original position. They are equal because each possesses the two moral powers. What makes the global original position—in which peoples are equal and persons therefore are not—different from the domestic original position?[16] The promised warrants are nowhere to be found in Rawls's explicit arguments. For all he has said, his arguments for the freedom and equality of persons remain as convincing as ever.

It might well seem not only *inconsistent* with the moral argument in *A Theory of Justice* to begin with peoples at the global level, but also simply *odd*. Peoples have no independent reality apart from the actual persons they comprise. The point of a theory of justice, at any level of society, will be to foster important aspects of actual persons' welfare and to safeguard against very serious wrongs to them. If it is the interests of actual persons that are in view, it might seem natural to treat actual persons as foundationally important globally. And doing so might seem especially important given that someone might well not regard a people, even a liberal people, that asserted jurisdiction over her as treating her fairly or as entitled to represent her or to make or enforce the rules governing her cooperation with others. A global system assuming the legitimacy of decent nonliberal peoples seems to beg the question against this sort of dissident and to rule out any sort of global order significantly more complex and pluralistic than the one currently in effect.[17]

## IV. Rawls's Actual Arguments for the Equality of Peoples Are Limited and Unconvincing

### A. *Rawls Offers a Cluster of Unpersuasive Arguments for the Global Equality of Peoples*

What Rawls actually says in defense of the equality of peoples gives us little reason to embrace his position. He notes that he treats peoples as equal members of global society because that is how they are viewed at present, thus making it difficult to see how one might mount a critique of the contemporary global order in Rawlsian terms (Section B). He implies that his clarification of the meaning of "people" should help to warrant his decision to treat peoples equally, but it doesn't (Section C). He maintains that a commitment to toleration presupposes the equality of persons, even though toleration needs to be justified and even though toleration seems perfectly possible on cosmopolitan grounds (Section D). Equality is, he maintains, a precondition for the self-respect of decent nonliberal peoples, but he has not shown that the requisite sort of self-respect is something on which an account of global justice should build (Section E). He rightly points out that nonegalitarians can be treated equally by egalitarians without inconsistency, but noting this does little to establish his general case for the equality of peoples (Section F). He suggests plausibly that particularized responsibility for assets and resources ensures that they will be well taken care of, but this point can be acknowledged and defended without any appeal to the equality of persons (Section G). Rawls's defenses of the global equality of peoples don't seem convincing (Section H).

## B. That Peoples Are Equal in Current Global Society Doesn't Mean They Should Be Treated That Way to the Detriment of Persons

Rawls seems to me only to compound the problem by maintaining that "[i]n the Law of Peoples ... we view *peoples* as conceiving of themselves as free and equal *peoples* in the Society of Peoples."[18] Thus, current global society, in which *peoples* theoretically conceive of themselves as equals, is treated as a given.[19] There may be any number of pragmatic reasons not to disturb the existing global order when *implementing* a given theory of justice, but there seems to be no excuse for viewing that order in the way Rawls does when *formulating* his theory unless the equality of peoples is itself theoretically necessary. In fact, however, he offers the reader little reason to join him in treating the current equality of peoples in global society as morally significant or, more generally, in treating peoples as essentially equal.

## C. Clarifying the Nature of Peoples Isn't Enough to Show That They Should Be Treated as Globally Foundational

Rawls says that §2 of *The Law of Peoples* contains a partial explanation of why a Rawlsian Law of Peoples is grounded in a procedure "that is fair to peoples and not to individual persons."[20] But §2 provides little assistance to the puzzled reader.

In this section, Rawls spells out the idea of a people as a group with a shared cultural identity, united by common sympathy and loyalty to a set of public institutions and norms of fairness.[21] I will assume *arguendo* that these characteristics explain why peoples *matter*, why they have morally relevant value, and why liberal peoples—which recognize this value and which are, in any case, committed to norms of respect—would show appropriate regard for other peoples, both liberal and nonliberal. But what Rawls says about the nature of a people serves at best to lay the groundwork for his later argument. Explaining what peoples *are* and why they might matter is not the same as showing that their interests ought to *trump* those of the particular persons who are their members. What Rawls says about freedom and equality at the domestic level provides some reason to embrace the view that persons are morally equal quite apart from their membership in particular societies (and Rawls might be seen as acknowledging this by choosing to respond to cosmopolitan challenges to his position). His simple *explanation* of the nature of peoples does not undermine his *argument* for the freedom and equality of persons in general or for the contention that persons should not be asked to sacrifice themselves for the well-being of their societies.

### D. The Equality of Peoples Can't Be Effectively Defended on the Basis That It Is Required as a Condition of Toleration

Rawls also suggests that some observations he makes in §11, while arguing for liberal tolerance of decent nonliberal peoples, help to explain why a Rawlsian Law of Peoples should be preferred to a Law of Persons.[22] Because advocating a cosmopolitan approach "amounts to saying that all persons are to have the equal liberal rights of citizens in a constitutional democracy,"[23] a cosmopolitan account of global justice would require liberal societies to seek (even if slowly and peaceably) to convert all other societies to liberalism.[24] We shouldn't endorse such a requirement unless we are sure that nonliberal societies don't meet the grade, something we would know only in view of "a reasonable liberal Law of Peoples."[25]

Such considerations, Rawls implies, justify the decision not to treat persons as equal in the course of formulating norms of global justice. The most fundamental problem with this claim is that Rawls hasn't shown that we have any particular reason to be tolerant in the first place. Presumably we need something like a Law of Peoples (or, better, a Law of Persons) to ground an account of global tolerance. So Rawls can't appeal to the value of tolerance to explain why such a Law should take the form he thinks it should. Put that concern to one side, however. It should still be clear that Rawls's hasn't shown that, if we assume that tolerance is important, we should treat peoples as equal and globally foundational.

Rawls's concern with tolerance can be seen as comprising at least two distinguishable elements: (*i*) liberals should not regard decent nonliberal societies as unjust because doing so would be disrespectful to the members of those societies, and (*ii*) liberals should not regard decent nonliberal societies as unjust because doing so might seem to justify forcible interference with these societies. But concern doesn't seem finally warranted on either front.

Rawls says that, in virtue of a cosmopolitan Law as he interprets it, liberals would deny "a due measure of respect"[26] to nonliberal peoples. But what is at issue is precisely what level of respect *is* due to nonliberal public institutions and cultural patterns. Whether liberal societies ought to tolerate decent nonliberal ones in this (or any other) sense would seem to be dependent on a satisfactory theory of justice; thus, a requirement of tolerance is best seen as a conclusion drawn from a satisfactory theory of justice, not as a constraint on what could count as such a theory. Even if not required at the most fundamental theoretical level, of course, tolerance of one sort or another might well be a demand of prudence or justice in the real world, but to show that it was would not be at the same time to show that it needed to be treated as a desideratum of a theory of global justice.

Rawls needs to distinguish between the different senses in which liberals might be said to show, or fail to show, respect for nonliberal peoples.[27] Regarding the institutions of decent nonliberal peoples as acting unjustly is quite compatible with refusing to humiliate such peoples or show contempt for them, presuming, of course, that vigorous disagreement is not in principle disrespectful.

While he regards decent nonliberal societies as deficient in justice, Rawls does view them as potentially *legitimate*, and therefore as entitled not to be interfered with by force. But embracing a Law of Persons is quite consistent with endorsing a refusal to justify state military intervention or sanctions to change putatively decent societies' institutions. Liberal peoples could accept decent nonliberal peoples as members of international associations without requiring that they embrace liberal conceptions of human rights in order to qualify for membership. And liberal peoples could perfectly well regard the institutions of nonliberal peoples as deficient and unreasonable without using force against them even while treating particular *members* of those peoples as possessing the same dignity and rights as members of liberal societies. To embrace the conclusion that decent nonliberal societies are unjust is *not* to treat them as appropriate targets for invasion, sanctions, or anything of the sort by the governments of liberal societies.

Defending Rawls's noncosmopolitan starting point, Harry Gould argues that, given a cosmopolitan standard of justice, "decent hierarchical societies are ruled out [if not declared oxymoronic], and . . . an entire segment of the world" is dismissed as unjust.[28] A cosmopolitan standard is objectionable because it denies the "acceptability" and "dignity of all other types of societies than our own."[29]

It is not clear what sort of claim Gould is making. Is it one that liberals ought to accept *as liberals*? From the standpoint of a cosmopolitan theory of justice, Rawls's decent hierarchical societies would, indeed, count as *unjust*. By denying their members full social and legal equality and by declining to respect the full panoply of liberal rights, such societies would fail to meet the demands of justice.

Rawls is certainly not committed to holding that all extant regimes are equally just; one reason to articulate a theory of justice in the first place is presumably to provide a tool for evaluating existing regimes. Rawls believes that the version of liberalism he defends is ultimately reasonable in a way that competing nonliberal views are not.[30] (Indeed, this is surely part of what it means to affirm *any* normative view.[31]) And this surely entails the conclusion that negative evaluations of nonliberal regimes are, at least in principle, perfectly defensible. The fact that, if a given view is correct, contradictory views will be incorrect should be relatively obvious and noncontroversial. (And if one only regards one's theory as reasonable, but not as correct, there will still be many positions that clearly cannot qualify as reasonable.) Liberals and nonliberals will doubtless think of each other as mistaken in important ways, even if they take each other's dignity and value seriously. That a theory justifies liberals in believing there is something wrong with nonliberal practices should hardly be thought of as cause for embarrassment.[32]

Whatever Rawls says about liberals' stance in relation to decent nonliberal societies, he seems perfectly willing to classify "an entire segment of the world" as unjust.[33] He clearly condemns benevolent absolutisms (with qualifications) and outlaw states as unjust.[34] And he regards even well-ordered nonliberal societies as less just than liberal societies.[35] It would hardly be open to him to object to a global Law of Persons merely because a variety of regimes appeared to be unjust in its light, given that he himself clearly regards those regimes as unjust or, at any rate, deficient as regards justice.

### E. Preserving the Self-Respect of Decent Nonliberal Peoples Shouldn't Play a Foundational Role in Framing Norms of Global Justice

Rawls plausibly believes that decent nonliberal societies' public institutions and human rights protections would be inconsistent with a Law of Persons.[36] Judging nonliberal peoples to be unjust would have negative consequences for their self-respect; this, he implies, is one reason we ought not to embrace such a Law.[37]

This argument does nothing to show that persons are not equal for political purposes and that they are not entitled to equal status domestically and globally and to a range of basic liberties. In addition, it does not explain why the self-respect of (supporters of the *status quo* in) decent nonliberal societies matters, when the self-respect of (supporters of the *status quo* in) benevolent absolutisms and outlaw states, clearly deserving of Rawlsian criticism, does not—unless self-respect depends on acting morally. (If proper self-respect doesn't depend on acting justly, then characterizing decent nonliberal peoples as unjust ought not to hamper their self-respect.) Liberal criticisms might adversely affect the self-respect of some persons in these societies, but this fact—rightly—fails to persuade Rawls that liberals should avoid criticizing them. And if self-respect depends on acting justly, there's no obvious reason the self-respect of decent nonliberal peoples *shouldn't* be called into question to the extent that their practices and institutions are unjust.[38] If proper self-respect depends on acting justly, then those who do act unjustly are, to the extent that they don't, not entitled to self-respect. So the fact that a particular conception of justice might make some people subject to criticism is not, on its own, a reason not to embrace that conception of justice. The fact that a cosmopolitan conception of justice might entail the indefensibility of some practices in decent nonliberal societies might explain why Rawlsian deliberators wouldn't embrace such a conception, but it wouldn't explain why a Rawlsian as opposed to a cosmopolitan conception of global justice should be preferred in the first place.

Perhaps the issue isn't whether decent nonliberal peoples are *entitled* to self-respect, but whether self-respect is *proper*. Suppose we think of it as simply a kind of natural fact—as, say, a matter of feeling good about oneself.[39] In this case, one might say that being subjected to criticism undermined self-respect and that this fact could be seen as a datum that could be used to generate moral constraints. But there seem to be several difficulties with this sort of defense of Rawls's approach: (*i*) Self-respect in the unmoralized sense hardly seems worth protecting. (*ii*) In addition, even if acknowledging the (putative) importance of this sort of self-respect could yield a presumption against certain sorts of criticism, this would not seem sufficient to show that the presumption couldn't be defeated. Just because it proved to be important not to undermine self-respect in this sense, it wouldn't follow that not doing so was *so* important that this provided a reason not to take the interests of particular persons into account.

Further, (*iii*) whether I ought to voice a given sort of criticism or condemnation in light of a given moral standard is a different question from whether the standard obtains in the first place; it would be perfectly compatible with acknowledging the force of the standard to avoid engaging in certain sorts of critical behavior in relation to decent nonliberal societies. There might be good reason

for liberals not to *announce* their disapproval of decent nonliberal peoples, but that they ought not to do this is irrelevant to the question whether the institutions of such peoples *merit* disapproval.[40]
Finally, (*iv*) it's important to be clear about *whose* self-respect is likely to be affected by the conclusion that decent nonliberal societies are unjust. There is no such thing as collective societal self-respect; there is only the self-respect of particular agents. The interest in self-respect grounded in group identity is plausibly understood as an interest of particular persons, if for no other reason than that only *sentients* have interests—that groups don't have interests that aren't the interests of the particular persons who constitute them. A person may respect herself as (among other things) a member of a particular group, and all the members of a group may do so. But to talk about the self-respect of the group is just to talk about the self-respect of the group's members, not to posit a conscious subject distinguishable from those members. And, at least ordinarily, group identity is merely one contributor to the good of personal self-respect. It is unlikely to be a master good that subsumes or trumps all the other primary goods that individual deliberators might acknowledge.[41]

Conduct that criticized the institutions and practices of decent nonliberal societies might undermine the self-respect (in the relevant nonmoral sense) of those committed to upholding the *status quo* on those societies; but, depending on how it was articulated, it certainly need not hamper the self-respect of those interested in fostering change (which might be enhanced by external pressures for liberalization and diminished by internal disregard for human rights). Indeed, the self-respect of citizens of decent nonliberal societies who wanted reforms that would make their societies more liberal might well be enhanced by the recognition that justice was on their side. Why should the interest nonliberal societies' dominant players and their supporters might have in preserving their self-respect trump the interest of other members of those societies in freedom and equality?

Individual deliberators might affirm the value of self-respect rooted in group membership. They might acknowledge reasons for tolerating decent nonliberal societies. But the appropriateness of these judgments would still be a function of the individual interests at stake, interests whose independence and value are effectively represented by means of a cosmopolitan second original position and reflected in a Law of Persons. Rawls has not shown that recognizing the liberal rights of all persons would necessarily do great harm to the reasonable self-respect of particular peoples. He has also failed to show convincingly why a people's interest in preserving its identity and self-respect trumps the interests of any of its individual members in something approximating the full panoply of liberal rights.[42] His argument from the value of self-respect does not warrant basing norms of global justice on the conclusions of Rawlsian deliberators rather than individual deliberators.[43]

### F. Nonegalitarian Institutions Can Be Treated as Equal to Egalitarian Institutions, but the Question Is Whether They Should Be

Rawls considers the objection that, because decent nonliberal societies are not egalitarian, they should not be entitled to equal representation. In response, he maintains, reasonably enough, that this is on its face a *non sequitur*, given that we treat groups with different organizational patterns (churches, say, or universities) as equal for certain purposes.[44] But rebutting one objection to his model is not the same as offering any persuasive reason for adopting the device of an original position in which peoples rather than individual persons deliberate.

### G. Allocated Responsibility Matters but Doesn't Require the Equality of Peoples

Rawls can also be seen as emphasizing that *someone* needs to be given responsibility for the world's resources in the absence of a global government and thus as opting for individual peoples as the remaining possible loci of responsibility.[45] The relationship between a government and its territory might, he thinks, be seen as comparable to a person's relationship to a valuable asset that is her property.[46]

However, an argument from the need for allocated responsibility would not warrant basing norms of global justice on the conclusions of Rawlsian rather than individual deliberators.[47] Allocated responsibility is compatible with the acceptance of global norms of justice just as individual property is compatible with, and, indeed (at least in the case, for Rawls, of personal property), required, by Rawlsian domestic justice.

For all I have so far argued, cosmopolitan deliberators might opt to endorse something like a global Society of Peoples. Or they might opt for some sort of state-free global environment. Either of these options could provide for allocated responsibility for resources. Thus, the argument shows why it might make sense to take peoples seriously. The argument does not show why, from a normative perspective, peoples, rather than persons, should be the building blocks of the global order. It does not suffice, therefore, to defeat the liberal presumption in favor of cosmopolitanism.

## H. Rawls Fails to Warrant the Treatment of Equal Peoples as Globally Foundational

Rawls offers little real argument for treating peoples, rather than persons, as basic at the global level.[48] He notes the equality of peoples (really, of course, states) in contemporary global society; but whether this equality ought to be preserved is precisely the question at issue. His clarification of the meaning of "people" doesn't bolster his case. He appeals unpersuasively—and, again, question-beggingly—to the liberal value of tolerance and implies that a system of cosmopolitan norms of global justice would be unappealingly intolerant. He suggests that what I am calling a Law of Persons would be inappropriate because it would require the pursuit of policies damaging to the self-respect of decent nonliberal peoples. He plausibly undermines the claim that intolerant regimes lose the right to be tolerated simply in virtue of their intolerance, but his having done so provides no positive reason for endorsing a Rawlsian Law of Peoples. He rightly emphasizes the need for allocated responsibility for resources and assets without showing that acknowledging the importance of such responsibility requires treating the equality of peoples as globally foundational. None of his arguments justifies rejecting the intuitively attractive view that the second original position should be structured in a way that is fair to free and equal persons.

## V. Rawls's Explicit Arguments Are Weak

Rawls recognizes that he needs to explain what is wrong with the cosmopolitan position, but his efforts to undermine it in *The Law of Peoples* seem relatively thin.

There is, one might have thought, a Rawlsian case to be made for the essential *moral* equality of all persons on the planet in virtue of their possession of the two moral powers.[49] That there is leaves open, of course, the question whether there is also a case for an equality among citizens of a particular state, members of a particular people, that distinguishes them from others. But someone who acknowledged a fellow citizen as equal because of her possession of the two moral powers might well, if confronted with a member of another people with those same powers, see her as equal in moral worth. And this might in turn prompt the thought that, in virtue of their moral equality, all persons on our planet should be entitled to equal representation in a global original position. Rawls notes the obviousness of this sort of argument, but he rejects it without careful explicit consideration.[50]

He acknowledges that his Law of Peoples is grounded in "an original position at the second level that is fair to peoples and not to individual persons."[51] But he does very little to defend his people-based starting point for reflection on global justice. He briskly rejects the global equality of persons and offers relatively undeveloped and insubstantial arguments for the foundational role he assigns to peoples at the global level. It is hard not to sympathize with Fernando Tesón's criticism that abandoning the equality of persons at the global level is simply "an *ad hoc* hypothesis"[52] that enables Rawls "to reach the results that he has *in advance* decided are the most plausible for the law of nations."[53] As even a defender of Rawls's position acknowledges, "[c]ertainly, his actual arguments about the differences between the domestic and the global are not an adequate justification" for his anticosmopolitanism.[54] But it may be that better Rawlsian justifications are available: there might be significant disanalogies between global and domestic society, and there might be good reason to think of membership in a given people as a characteristic of foundational moral importance. In Chapter 3, I consider, and reject, several potential justifications for treating peoples as foundational at the global level.

CHAPTER 3

# Challenging the Global Primacy of Peoples

### I. Additional Arguments Can Be Offered for the Foundational Role of Peoples at the Global Level, though None Should Be Seen as Undermining Cosmopolitanism

Despite the relative thinness of Rawls's own explicit arguments in *The Law of Peoples* for treating peoples (or states—I use the terms interchangeably here) as foundational at the global level, alternative defenses of his position are available. I doubt, however, that any provides good reason to embrace Rawlsian statism rather than cosmopolitanism. A Law of Persons could ground a fair, cooperative global venture for mutual advantage (allowing for a suitably nuanced conception of what it might mean to talk about a society as a venture)—and might merit the loyalty of the world's people even if it didn't (Part II). Such a Law could achieve public justification and could, in any case, bind in the absence of the legitimacy conferred by such justification (Part III). States are not inescapable and basic features of the world scene that any account of global justice must treat as foundational (Part IV). The relativist dismissal of commitments to freedom and equality as contingent features of Western liberal thought need not count against cosmopolitan liberalism (Part V). There is good reason to affirm cosmopolitanism despite multiple objections (Part VI).

## II. A Cosmopolitan Global Society Could Qualify as a Fair Cooperative Venture for Mutual Advantage

### A. Global Society Could Be a Fair Cooperative Venture

In the absence of a world state, a global society could still count as a fair cooperative venture for mutual advantage, depending on how such a venture is understood. Such a society already links people across state boundaries in mutually beneficial relationships, and it could do so even more effectively if states didn't work to impede global interchange (Section B). It could count as a *fair* system of cooperation even in the absence of a global government (Section C). The viability of a Rawlsian approach should not be seen as turning, at least at the global level, on the existence of an *actual* scheme of fair cooperation, which suggests that Rawlsian standards as regards what is to count as a fair system of cooperation need not be unduly high (Section D). Cosmopolitanism should not be ruled out by concerns about the viability of a global scheme of fair cooperation (Section E).

### B. A Global Society Could Be a Cooperative Venture for Mutual Advantage

In virtue of the various interconnections that link people across the planet, global society can be understood as a cooperative venture for mutual advantage. Understanding it in this way could help to blunt one sort of Rawlsian objection to treating all persons as morally and politically equal. There are reasons to qualify talk about global society, or any domestic society, as a single venture; it is more reasonable, I will subsequently suggest, to talk about multiple ventures, about overlapping networks of cooperation, rather than a unified cooperative activity. But it is possible to give a not unreasonable sense to talk about global society as a cooperative venture in a way that can be seen as offering some purchase to talk about global justice in Rawlsian terms.

Rawls argues for the equality of persons at the domestic level in virtue of their possession of the two moral powers. But, of course, in *A Theory of Justice* he doesn't address the question whether the citizens of a given state are equal to citizens of other states; he treats the state as self-contained. The simple fact that people are, by hypothesis, equal as members of a given polity does not entail the conclusion that political institutions should treat them as equal with all other persons in the world. Rawls takes the existing nation-state system largely for granted, despite his preference for talk of "peoples" rather than "states." He might be thought to do so in *A Theory of Justice* particularly because of his conception of a society as a cooperative venture for mutual advantage. The bounds of a society—within which equality among persons matters and should be presupposed—follow from the extent of this cooperative venture. People engaged in such a venture share a common fate, confront many of the same general risks, and so forth. So, on this view, it makes sense that it should be those engaged in such a venture, rather than others with whom they might be thought to have little connection, who should ask whether their possession of the two moral powers, along with their common subjection to similar circumstances and their mutual interdependence, might not justify their treatment of one another as equals, and so warrant the device of the original position as a way of representing their fundamental moral and political relationship with one another.

While all persons, by definition, possess the basic moral requisites for equality with one another, one might suppose a plausible Rawlsian view to be that political institutions need not be designed in light of each person's equality with all others, per se, but only in light of her equality with the others engaged in the cooperative venture that is her society. Because a global society is not such a venture, the moral equality of individual persons need not be reflected in such a society's institutions and rules.[1]

This rejoinder to the sort of moral and political egalitarianism that might seem readily defensible in Rawlsian terms is intriguing, but it need not be seen as decisive.

Whether a given domestic polity really is a cooperative venture (for mutual advantage or otherwise) is surely not an all-or-nothing affair. People cooperate with and depend on one another in a variety of ways and to a variety of degrees. There is no bright-line rule (other than one that simply refers to state-made borders) that distinguishes the cooperation in which two members of a given polity engage from the cooperation in which one of them might engage with a member of a different polity.

There is often (though not always, and not necessarily) more cooperation among members of a given polity than among any of them and members of other polities. But this is not a natural fact that helps define the boundaries of a society as a cooperative venture for mutual advantage. Instead, it is, characteristically, a consequence of the existence of states with boundaries—states that seek in various ways to constrain cross-border cooperation. Cooperation certainly takes place despite these constraints, and it would take place much more readily in their absence.

Indeed, if we think of wide-ranging cooperation as both persistently beneficial and morally attractive, we might see its increasing realization as a morally appealing aspiration. And the recognition of this aspiration as attractive might well lead us precisely not to reify state boundaries as setting constraints on the extent of cooperation. Treating a state as a self-contained cooperative venture seems likely to help to keep the state self-contained; a more expansive conception of the potential for cooperation should tend, in turn, to foster its own realization.

In any event, as I have suggested, even in a world in which states are treated as fundamental, extensive cooperation and interdependence across state borders persist.[2] People across our planet join one another, deliberately and anonymously, in a broad range of cultural and economic and social activities. The globe is not the same kind of cooperative venture as an isolated small town; but neither, of course, is any modern nation-state. If a typical modern nation-state is reasonably treated as a cooperative venture in Rawlsian terms, then refusing to treat the globe as a whole as such a venture seems relatively arbitrary—particularly given that the potential for cooperation would be much greater in the absence of state-imposed barriers. After all, cooperation need not be seen merely as a precondition for the establishment of Rawlsian justice but also, surely, as among its goals. An account of justice that treats people as moral equals despite accidents of geography can be warranted both in virtue of this potential and as a means of realizing it.

Provided venture language is not pressed too far, global society can be seen as a cooperative venture for mutual advantage, differing at most in degree from smaller, local societies.[3] Treating the presumptive equal members of that society as individually equal for purposes of formulating a theory of justice thus seems, at first blush, perfectly defensible.[4] And, indeed, it is (for the nonce) global society, and only global society, that qualifies as "a closed system,"[5] membership in which is bounded only by birth and death.[6] The kind of cohesion Rawls envisions as characteristic of the society whose representatives deliberate in the original position is arguably possessed only by global society.[7]

Global society seems, at least at first blush, to qualify as a cooperative venture for mutual advantage—at least if *venture* is understood in a sufficiently open-textured manner (as it almost certainly should be at the domestic level, too).

### C. Global Society, Understood as a Cooperative Venture, Could Qualify as Fair

#### 1. A Law of Persons Could Ground a Fair System of Global Cooperation

Fairness could be a feature of a global society adhering to a Law of Persons. It might be thought that a global state or similar institution would be required for a global society to count as a genuinely *fair* system of cooperation (Subsection 2). There is good reason not to want a global state, and the viability of cosmopolitanism does not depend on such a state (Subsection 3). Various sorts of order-maintenance mechanisms for global legal norms could be employed in the absence of a world state (Subsection 4). A global legal order could enjoy significant support without the existence and operation of a global government (Subsection 5). Enforcement would be a problem for a Rawlsian Law of Peoples, which means that a Rawlsian critic of a Law of Persons shouldn't articulate unduly high enforcement expectations for a cosmopolitan legal order (Subsection 6). A global society operating in accordance with a Law of Persons could qualify as a reasonably fair system of cooperation (Subsection 7).

#### 2. A Global State Might Be Thought Necessary to Render Global Society a Fair System of Cooperation

For Rawls, a just society is, among other things, a *fair* system of cooperation.[8] A society counts as such a system if the following requirements are met: (*i*) people generally act in accordance with suitable regulative norms; (*ii*) these norms are to some extent internalized (and do not need constantly to be backed up with the threat of punitive sanctions); (*iii*) these rules are designed, at least in principle, to foster the good of each participant; and (*iv*) social interactions are designed to be reciprocally or mutually beneficial.[9] The use of coercive authority to coordinate the behavior of otherwise independent actors is not *sufficient* to render a system of cooperation fair.[10] But a Rawlsian might nonetheless regard it as *necessary*. A Society of Peoples, he might argue, could be just to persons—could be a fair cooperative venture among them— only if a world government existed. Absent such a government,[11] responsibility for the enforcement of global legal norms would rest largely with local institutions of various sorts. And since a Law of Persons would constrain the activities of a given people while limiting the pursuit of its members' shared objectives, individual peoples would be willing to implement it fitfully at best. Without consistent support from authorities with the power to implement a Law of Persons, it would be inconsistently applied, because peoples and individuals would be too prone to ignore its requirements, and the Society of Peoples would not qualify as a fair system of cooperation.[12] A Law of Persons might be thought not to bind under such circumstances.

## 3. Cosmopolitanism Does Not Presuppose a World State

A cosmopolitan starting point can't reasonably be rejected on the basis that it would require the creation of a global state.

There is surely reason to squirm, at least a little, when Véronique Zanetti, defending a cosmopolitan starting point for global law, bemoans the absence of "a monopoly of power" at the global level and of the "instruments necessary for [the] implementation," presumably coercive, of global principles of distributive justice.[13] The amount of power an authority with the kind of power Zanetti envisions would surely be troubling, and conferring this sort of power on any entity seems risky. (And, of course, the sorts of worries evoked by Zanetti's enthusiasm for a monopolistic hegemon point to serious problems with smaller territorially monopolistic states as well, *absent* ease of exit and the resulting possibility of a Tiebout competition [in which freedom of movement fosters institutional change because people are able to relocate to avoid unappealing institutions and policies and to seek to live under more appealing ones], and so provide some support for the anarchic alternative I defend in Chapter 5.)

But the appropriateness of a Law of Persons does not turn on the attractiveness or viability of a unitary world government. The viability of a world government would affect the appropriateness of such a Law in only two cases: (*i*) if we assumed that individual deliberators would *necessarily* opt for a world government or (*ii*) if the idea of a Law of Persons were reasonable only on the assumption that a world government existed. Neither assumption is plausible.

Individual deliberators at the global level subject to the same Rawlsian constraints as individual deliberators at the domestic level would embrace the same kinds of norms, presumably, as their domestic counterparts. They could be expected to adopt similar principles regarding the design of institutions affecting the distribution of wealth. They would doubtless opt for extensive human rights protections. They would likely also establish global rules affecting certain kinds of institutions.[14] But it does not follow that they would opt for a world government.[15]

Suppose there were, as I take there to be, good reasons not to want a global government. In this case, individual deliberators at the global level could perfectly well opt against such a government. There is no artificial feature of a cosmopolitan original position that would *require* them to opt for a unitary world government, or, indeed, any sort of government at all. They could reasonably take into account any tendencies inherent in human social life or individual psychology that might lead to doubts about centralized power. If a global government proved either nonviable or unattractive, as it likely would, they clearly would not conclude that justice required its creation.

### 4. Multiple Means of Maintaining Order Are Conceivable Absent a World State

It is simply not clear that states are necessarily as important in the current global order as arguments for a state-based or people-based approach to global justice might appear to assume.[16] A variety of nonstate institutions could help to secure support for a Law of Persons in the absence of a global government; these might include organizations formed to foster cooperation among peoples, organizations linking agencies in particular governments, nongovernmental organizations of various kinds, and commercial entities. The governments of existing peoples, as long as they existed, could also be envisioned as playing useful roles. The result might not be, and presumably would not be, a uniform global legal system. But it is not unreasonable to expect convergence on a variety of fundamental legal norms, even as diverse territorial or nonterritorial legal systems continued to exhibit significant diversity. Provided central norms were consistently upheld, fair cooperation would be possible.

It is important to stress that the availability of *enforcement* mechanisms is not obviously the most salient issue here. "Like most laws, international rules are rarely enforced, but usually obeyed."[17] There is some evidence that governments adhere to at least some norms because they perceive these norms to be fair.[18] And domestic legal systems regularly internalize global legal norms even in the absence of relevant global enforcement mechanisms.[19] Thus, the absence of a global government would not keep a global society grounded in a Law of Persons from functioning as a fair system of cooperation.

*5. Limited but Significant Support for a Law of Persons Could Be Achieved*
There is an obvious Rawlsian objection to arguments focusing on alternatives to a global government and on the parity between a Rawlsian Law of Peoples and a Law of Persons. The objector can grant the potential existence of institutions that might help to implement a Law of Persons absent a global government and despite the formal parity between such a Law and a Rawlsian Law of Peoples. But, she might argue, this misses the point: the ability of a Law of Persons to ground a fair system of cooperation would be limited, given the likelihood of widespread opposition to what nonliberals would regard as its radical features. But a Law of

Persons could enjoy more support than a Rawlsian objector might initially suppose.[20]

Even if uniform or majority support for a Law of Persons did not immediately emerge, support for it could continue to prove sufficiently stable to ground a system of cooperative interaction between persons and across individual societies.[21] Potential instability need not prevent it from grounding a fair system of cooperation, even if stability is a requisite of such a system. Rawls grants, after all, that a substantial number of peoples may well not endorse a Rawlsian Law of Peoples. He does not seem to regard this possibility as justifying the further attenuation of his proposed Law of Peoples, however. Indeed, he acknowledges elsewhere that "a just scheme of cooperation may not be in equilibrium, much less stable."[22]

Rawls does not suggest that the Law of Peoples be reframed to secure the support of outlaw states or benevolent absolutisms, whatever their numbers or influence. And it would be odd if he did so. Under ordinary circumstances, it would be extremely difficult to enact or enforce a public policy in a liberal society without the support of the wealthy. But he does not, in the interests of stability, accord their voices or interests extra weight when designing the domestic original position. It makes no more sense for Rawlsians to treat peoples rather than persons fairly when designing the second original position.

Even though only cosmopolitan liberals may at first wholeheartedly endorse the principles of a Law of Persons, this need not mean that a global regime embodying such a Law would enjoy so little support from decent nonliberals that it would be too unstable to serve as a system of fair cooperation. Decent nonliberals could certainly endorse many of the provisions of a Law of Persons. Assuming a Rawlsian Law of Peoples would be stable, it seems as if the stability of a Law of Persons would be threatened, if at all, only when it yielded requirements different from those contained in a Rawlsian Law of Peoples.

A Law of Persons *would*, of course, yield some requirements that would be unlikely to attract the support of decent nonliberals (not to mention benevolent absolutisms and outlaw states), and indeed, if my proposals regarding its content were accepted, some liberal societies would doubtless object as well. But this fact need not affect adherence to norms that aren't in dispute. And the overall stability of support for a Law of Persons might be such that a measure of dissent from certain features of such a Law would not lead to significant upset. Peoples that did not find individual features of a Law of Persons attractive might nonetheless support them because doing so reduced domestic discontent—many members of their societies might, after all, respond positively to increased liberalization. And the overall stability of a global order shaped by a Law of Persons might contain the effects of dissent regarding particular, more controversial norms. So it would be difficult to mount a Rawlsian argument against a Law of Persons on the basis that a global society grounded in such a Law could not count as such a system of cooperation.

*6. Because Enforcement Would Pose Problems for a Law of Peoples as Well as a Law of Persons, Consistent Actual Enforcement Might Not Be a Requirement for a Law of Persons to Be Fair on Rawlsian Terms*
The absence of a global government might be seen as creating potential problems for a Rawlsian Law of Peoples just as it would for a Law of Persons. If a Rawlsian Law of Peoples could count as a fair system of cooperation in the absence of a world government, this provides added reason to suppose that a cosmopolitan Society of Peoples could as well.

Suppose individual societies *are* centrally important. If this is so, the fact that it is could create difficulties for a Rawlsian Society of Peoples just as it could for a global society grounded in a Law of Persons. If a world government did not exist, there might still be Rawlsian grounds for regarding the requirements embodied in a Law of Peoples as fair. But it is not clear that a Rawlsian Society of Peoples would be any better at *ensuring* that these requirements were actually implemented than would a Law of Persons.[23] Depending on just what institutional arrangements obtained, the absence of such a government might leave militarily or economically strong peoples free to be more abusive to weak peoples than they could be if such a government obtained. Societies might well seek to shirk their putative obligations under the Law of Peoples.[24]

A Rawlsian might argue that questions of fairness arise under circumstances in which there is already widespread acceptance of a Law of Peoples; but if full or at least frequent compliance can be treated as a *premise*, then it is reasonable to assume that a Law of Persons would ground to a fair system of cooperation as well. If most or all people adhered to a Law of Persons, all would be in a position to reap its benefits without excessive cost. As Rawls conceives of the Society of Peoples, it is clearly a fair cooperative venture for mutual advantage. Thus, to imply that a cosmopolitan Society of Peoples minus a world government would not be such a venture would be at the same time to imply that the Society of Peoples *he* imagines wouldn't be either.

A global order shaped by a Rawlsian Law of Peoples might be unstable even if liberal and decent nonliberal peoples endorsed the Law of Peoples, given that significant numbers of other peoples might not endorse it. But the empirical extent of the likely support available for a Rawlsian Law of Peoples need not be seen as decisively determining whether the operation of such a Law would be fair or not. Despite the potential lack of widespread support for a Rawlsian Law of Peoples, such a Law could still serve as a fair system of cooperation. A similar lack of support, then, need not count against the defensibility of a global Law of Persons.

*7. The Achievement of Reasonably Fair Cooperation in Accordance with a Law of Persons Seems Like a Viable Possibility*

A global society grounded in a Law of Persons could feature fair cooperation in a way that would make talk about justice within it meaningful.

There is certainly reason to be doubtful about a global government. But such a government is not required for a global society to qualify as a fair system of cooperation (or, better, as an array of networks of fair cooperation). And, in any case, at least some of the duties incumbent on persons and societies under a cosmopolitan or Rawlsian Law of Peoples would be binding, by Rawls's own lights, in the absence of a fair system of cooperation. Thus, fairness, rather than enforcement, seems to be the decisive factor. If I'm right, an objection to a Law of Persons based on the importance of ensuring that a Society of Peoples was a fair system of cooperation wouldn't rule out a cosmopolitan starting point for reflection on global justice.

A world government would not be required to enforce global legal norms. And it seems possible that such norms might enjoy significant support. A Law of Peoples might not be easy to enforce in the absence of a global government, which suggests that Rawlsian standards for fair cooperation ought not to be overly high. It would be unreasonable for Rawlsians to hold proponents of a Law of Persons to a higher standard than those to which Rawlsians hold themselves.

A global society grounded in a Law of Persons could, indeed, be a fair cooperative venture, provided the notion of a "venture" is sufficiently nuanced, as it should be at the domestic level as well. It would feature mechanisms designed to foster cooperation even in the absence of a global government, and it could reasonably be expected to attract significant support.

### D. *Duties May Obtain in the Absence of Fair Cooperation*

It is unclear that the norms of a Rawlsian political morality can be understood to apply only in circumstances marked by fair cooperation. Rawls makes clear with respect to transnational moral duties that a number of the requirements of his political morality hold in the absence of a fair system of cooperation. So the bounds of fair cooperation and the bounds of duty would not seem to be coextensive.

Rawls clearly believes that the Law of Peoples obligates individuals in the absence of a global government. He notes that the duty to respect the human rights safeguarded by the Law of Peoples "extends to all societies" and binds "all peoples and societies, including outlaw states."[25] Among the principles making up his proposed Law of Peoples is the requirement that peoples respect limits on the use of force,[26] and he seems to suppose that these restrictions bind *individuals*.[27] Discussing the norms of war in *A Theory of Justice*, he suggests that, in the second original position, "the traditional prohibitions incorporating the natural duties that protect human life would be chosen."[28]

[C]onscientious refusal in time of war . . . is based upon the same theory of justice that underlies the [domestic] constitution and guides its interpretation. Moreover, the legal order itself presumably recognizes in the form of treaties the validity of at least some of [the traditional] principles of the law of nations. Therefore if a soldier is ordered to engage in certain illicit acts of war, he may refuse if he reasonably and conscientiously believes that the principles applying to the conduct of war are plainly violated. He can maintain that, all things considered, his natural duty not to be made the agent of grave injustice and evil to another outweighs his duty to obey.[29]

Rawls appears here to envision a case in which an individual soldier refuses to commit an act because she regards it as inconsistent with the demands of morality *per se*.[30] There is no reference to a functioning Society of Peoples that might enforce these principles on all combatants. The requirements related to war, at any rate, are matters of "natural duty."[31] And natural duties "have no necessary connection with institutions or social practices."[32] They "are owed not only to definite individuals, say to those cooperating together in a particular social arrangement, but to persons generally."[33] Natural duties are derived from deliberation in the original position. But, given that they can be owed to, among others, noncombatants and enemy combatants in wartime, and that these people are likely to be citizens of other states, it follows either (*i*) that one need not be a participant in a cooperative venture for mutual advantage in order for one's interests to be considered in the first original position—that one need not be a deliberator at all—or (*ii*) that for some purposes the first original position is already cosmopolitan.

A Rawlsian Law of Peoples thus appears to bind individuals in at least some instances even absent any mechanism designed to secure general compliance with its demands. This implies *either* that the question whether a fair system of social cooperation exists is relevant to the validity of only *some* norms of justice *or* that global society can be a fair system of cooperation absent any unitary global enforcement mechanism. Of course, from the fact that some parts of the Law of Peoples are binding regardless of whether they can be expected to be enforced, it does not follow that *all* are. But it does follow that there is some reason to regard appeals to duties independent of enforcement mechanisms as consistent with a Rawlsian approach.[34]

### E. Affirming Cosmopolitanism Is Consistent with Regarding a Fair Cooperative Venture for Mutual Advantage as a Crucial Site of Justice

A global society structured in accordance with a Law of Persons could be a fair cooperative venture for mutual advantage, given a sufficiently textured conception of such a venture. There is an important sense in which global society already obtains. Even if it is not fair, it clearly *is* a cooperative venture (or an array of overlapping, interlocking cooperative ventures) for mutual advantage, and making it more cooperative, fairer, and more mutually advantageous seems like an appealing moral aspiration. Doing so wouldn't require that there be a world state—something we have good reason not to want. Alternative institutions could foster fair global cooperation, though there are Rawlsian reasons to think that defensible norms of global justice could obtain before such institutions were in place or fully functional. Thus, cosmopolitanism remains reasonable in the face of challenges focused on the need for a global scheme of fair cooperation as an alleged precondition for talk about global justice.

## III. A Cosmopolitan Global Society Could Achieve Public Justification but Could Qualify as Legitimate without It

### A. A Global Society Normed by a Law of Persons Could, but Need Not, Be Publicly Justified

Rawls came increasingly to stress the significance of overlapping consensus and public justification for the legitimacy of an account of political morality (Section B). A Rawlsian critique of a Law of Persons might suggest that such a Law couldn't be publicly justified and so couldn't qualify as legitimate (Section C). But a Law of Peoples might, indeed, be publicly justified (Section D). Rawls's preferred constructivist method in political philosophy need not be seen as undermining this conclusion (Section E). And public justification need not be seen as essential to the validity of basic norms of political morality like those that would form the core of a Law of Persons, which could exhibit legitimacy in the absence of public justification (Section F). A Law of Persons could thus be reasonably regarded as legitimate and as adequately justified (Section G).

### B. Rawls's Later Work Emphasizes the Importance of Overlapping Consensus and Public Justification

A relatively unsympathetic reading of Rawls's project in *The Law of Peoples* might treat it as an essentially *strategic* one: no theory of justice, per se, would be required for its implementation, though general agreement on the value of peace and cooperation would obviously be needed. But it seems clear that Rawls regards his project as normative and aspirational, not limited simply to the task of refining the principles implicit in current interstate relations. He describes himself as concerned to articulate an account of "right and justice" at the global level[35] and not merely to recommend helpful strategies for global comity. It may not be unreasonable, then, to reflect critically on the Law of Peoples as a potentially robust account of global *justice*. But, it might be argued, justice here has to be understood as a political conception in accord with the tenor of Rawls's later work. It is not clear that we need to accept Rawls's later recasting of his work; but it is, at any rate, worth asking to what extent accepting that recasting, *arguendo*, would mean opting against cosmopolitanism.

In *A Theory of Justice*, Rawls envisioned a political order in which justice as fairness was understood as a central element of a "comprehensive doctrine" organizing the moral as well as political lives of citizens.[36] But it was unrealistic, he subsequently concluded, to believe that, given the "fact of reasonable pluralism,"[37] people in a modern liberal society could be expected to unite in endorsing a single comprehensive doctrine.[38]

Rawls came to focus on *stability for the right reasons* and related ideas, including the notion of an *overlapping consensus* and the requirement of *public justification*, as essential features of a theory of domestic justice. If the stability of a society committed to justice as fairness were dependent on the existence of a consensus supporting a particular comprehensive doctrine, such a society simply wouldn't be stable in the relevant sense: the comprehensive doctrine couldn't be expected to enjoy widespread, self-reinforcing support. Justice as fairness would thus need to be defended as a "political conception," designed to provide a basis for fair cooperation within a diverse society. The later Rawls can be seen as appealing to moral considerations *as elements of the public culture of liberal societies*; normative argument in his later work may thus be seen as explicating the moral self-understanding of liberal societies rather than as offering any sort of ultimate rationale for that self-understanding.[39] The ideas of public justification, moral constructivism, and legitimacy play important roles in his new account of liberal political morality.

What warrants support for an account of justice in a given society is the ability of people with diverse fundamental views to find support for that account in light of the distinctive elements of their own particular views. Thus, justice as fairness at the domestic level can, on Rawls's view, be both legitimate and a source of stability only if convincing to people in light of their own preexisting (reasonable) views.[40] Rawls appears confident that justice as fairness can meet the test he has proposed, not least because he has reconceived it in constructivist terms as an elaboration of the existing political morality of liberal societies.

A politically liberal society whose institutions are framed in accordance with norms endorsed in the first original position would be stable, for Rawls, for two reasons: (*i*) People raised in a society endorsing such norms would tend to develop, and would have good reason to develop, the sense that institutions consistent with these norms were fair. (*ii*) A reasonable citizen in a liberal society would tend to support the norms created in the first original position on the basis of the reasonable comprehensive doctrine to which she adhered.[41]

Rawls intends his theory to be compatible with a wide range of alternative comprehensive doctrines. It is not meant, per se, to compete with such doctrines for popular allegiance. Justice as fairness can therefore, he believes, enjoy stable support even within a highly diverse society. Representatives of diverse ideological positions could endorse justice as fairness, because it is concerned only with the political realm, leaving people free to live out the tenets of their various comprehensive doctrines outside the political sphere (even though the political sphere is defined rather broadly).[42] The stability of justice as fairness as Rawls conceives it depends on the existence of an overlapping consensus of comprehensive doctrines. While representatives of diverse comprehensive doctrines might have very different reasons for regarding social institutions shaped by justice as fairness as reasonable, their respective doctrines might give each of them reason to view such institutions as deserving their support. The point is not that the norms endorsed in the first, domestic, original position would be determined by means of an empirical inquiry into the various comprehensive doctrines endorsed within a given society. Rather, Rawls simply wants to suggest that persons with a broad range of views could, despite their doctrinal differences, endorse the norms emerging from the original position.[43]

At the domestic level, Rawls supposes, justice as fairness would gradually be endorsed as its attractiveness became progressively more apparent. Initially, liberal institutions might be grudgingly tolerated as part of a constitutional settlement. Increasingly, politically liberal norms would be accepted appreciatively, without much theoretical support, as assumed features of the constitutional order. Finally, widespread affirmation of an overlapping consensus supporting politically liberal principles would emerge.[44] Rawls suggests that the pressures generated by a liberal constitutional order would tend to lead to the creation of a broader, principled commitment to political liberalism (and something approximating justice as fairness).[45] "[C]itizens who affirm the political conception [of justice], and who have been raised in and are familiar with the fundamental ideas of the public political culture, find that, when they adopt its framework of deliberation, their judgments converge sufficiently so that political cooperation on the basis of mutual respect can be maintained."[46]

Rawls emphasizes that his is not a "modus vivendi" position, in accordance with which a group unable to exercise commanding authority in a given society might endorse political liberalism as a matter of expediency.[47] "[A] balance of reasons as seen within each citizen's comprehensive doctrine, and not a compromise compelled by circumstances, is the basis of citizens' respect for the limits of public reason."[48] Justice as fairness would enjoy stable support because it is endorsed not out of expediency but out of principle.[49] A society rooted in justice as fairness would be stable because justice as fairness is a position "that aims at being acceptable to citizens as reasonable and rational, as well as free and equal, and so as addressed to their public reason."[50] Rawls distinguishes the "full justification" of such a view from "public justification."[51] On the one hand, "full justification is carried out by an individual citizen as a member of civil society . . . [as she] accepts a political conception and fills out its justification by embedding it . . . into . . . [her] comprehensive doctrine as either true or reasonable."[52] Rawls notes that "[s]ome [citizens] may consider the political conception *fully* justified even though it is not accepted by other people."[53] On the other hand, "*[p]ublic* justification happens when all the reasonable members of political society carry out a justification of the shared political conception by embedding it in their several reasonable comprehensive views."[54]

Determining if "an overlapping consensus on the political conception is possible is a way of checking whether there are sufficient reasons for proposing justice as fairness [as a doctrine] . . . which can be sincerely defended before others without criticizing or rejecting their deepest religious and philosophical commitments."[55] The existence of "adequate reasons for diverse reasonable people jointly to affirm justice as fairness as their working political conception" warrants "their legitimately exercising coercive political power over one another."[56]

### C. A Law of Persons Might Seem Indefensible because Incapable of Being Publicly Justified

A defender of Rawls's Law of Peoples might seek to argue that a global order grounded in a Law of Persons could not be publicly justified and would not enjoy the support of an overlapping consensus of reasonable comprehensive doctrines.[57] By contrast, it might be argued, a Rawlsian Law of Peoples *could* qualify as legitimate.[58]

Political liberalism is, Rawls seems to think, defensible at the domestic level because it enjoys the support of a consensus of reasonable comprehensive doctrines. Many of these doctrines are liberal, but even those that are not have been shaped by their adherents' experiences as members of a liberal society. Proponents of nonliberal comprehensive doctrines are likely, therefore, to recognize the merits of political liberalism as a framework for domestic *political* life, even if they dispute the claims of comprehensive liberalism as an account of *moral* and *cultural* life. Thus, the fact that a domestic consensus of reasonable comprehensive doctrines might come to exist in support of political liberalism is historically contingent.

A robustly liberal account of justice might be—as Rawls clearly thinks justice as fairness is—more reasonable than any alternative; nonetheless, it is perfectly possible that there might be societies in which many or most people adhered to comprehensive doctrines that provided little or no support for such an account of justice. Committed to various nonliberal ways of life, they will resent and resist the implications of a Law of Persons, which they will decline to endorse. Such a Law, therefore, will be unlikely to garner the support of an overlapping consensus of comprehensive doctrines.[59] "Since 'global citizens' cannot be assumed to view themselves as free and equal individuals who should relate fairly to each other across the board, we cannot build coercive social institutions which assume that they do."[60]

By contrast, a Rawlsian Law of Peoples might have a reasonable chance of gaining the support of a global consensus, with the result that enforcing it might be more clearly appropriate on Rawlsian grounds. Because such a Law would generally assume the existing norms of international law and the equality of peoples instead of challenging them, and would thus leave room for nonliberal societies to continue implementing nonliberal public policies, endorsing it would be far less difficult for most peoples on the basis of their comprehensive doctrines. A Rawlsian Law of Peoples could therefore be publicly justified, while a Law of Persons could not. A Rawlsian Law of Peoples would be legitimate, while a Law of Persons would be illegitimate.

## D. A Law of Persons Could Achieve Public Justification

### 1. There Might Be Multiple Paths to Public Justification for a Law of Persons

A cosmopolitan liberal might defend the claim that a Law of Persons would be endorsed by an overlapping consensus of reasonable comprehensive doctrines in several ways. She could suggest that such doctrines already overlap more than a critic might suppose—enough, in fact, that they might yield adequate support for a Law of Persons (Subsection 2). In parallel with the kind of domestic development Rawls envisions, an overlapping consensus in support of a Law of Persons could emerge over time after the initial embrace of such a Law and the gradual emergence of the necessary consensus could provide it with Rawlsian legitimacy (Subsection 3). She might seek to limit the relevant doctrines to ones that could, in fact, provide support for a Law of Persons (Subsection 4). She could thus maintain on multiple grounds that a Law of Persons could achieve public justification (Subsection 5).

### 2. A Law of Persons Might Prove to Be Supported by an Existing Consensus

The cosmopolitan liberal might maintain that, given the widespread influence of the Western media and the intrinsic appeal of liberal ideas, there is more global support for cosmopolitan liberalism than might immediately be supposed. While those in power in many of the world's societies might refuse to act in accordance with the norms contained in a Law of Persons, the cosmopolitan liberal need not show that she would support such a Law or conform her domestic policies, laws, and institutions to it. She need only show that, given the opportunity, a substantial majority of the world's people would endorse domestic and intersocietal institutions and norms consistent with a Law of Persons. Their support could be sufficiently widespread to ensure global legitimacy for cosmopolitan liberalism.

Perhaps the best defense for this view would be to maintain that "there is an expanding global culture of human rights that exhibits a broad consensus on the idea that justice requires respect for the inherent dignity of all persons, that this notion of dignity includes the idea that all persons are equal, so far as the importance of their basic interests [is] concerned, and that among the latter is an interest in freedom."[61] Official pundits in various nonliberal societies may praise the virtues of their societies' institutions, but this is no guarantee that their people would share their sentiments. The Western media have spread images of freedom and—if not often enough—equality of authority, rights, and status all over the world. The development of struggles for empowerment in a variety of authoritarian and totalitarian societies suggests that liberal ideas already enjoy some support in these societies—perhaps enough to ground significant support for cosmopolitan norms of global justice.

*3. A Consensus in Support of a Law of Persons Might Emerge as a Result of Cultural Shifts and Related Developments*
The cosmopolitan liberal could argue that support for a Law of Persons could develop over time. Rawls suggests, of course, that a similar kind of development might occur in the case of political liberalism at the domestic level.[62] Once in place, liberal principles of justice could generate their own bases of support.[63] They could be seen as responding effectively to the diverse convictions prevalent in the environment to which they apply, giving adherents of various comprehensive doctrines an opportunity to forge satisfactory relationships despite their disagreements.[64]

The principles of justice as fairness are—says Rawls—clearer and easier to apply than those of other, more complex and comprehensive positions, and they are thus more likely to be seen as attractive bases for an initial, "constitutional" consensus.[65] And when liberal principles (whether Rawls's or others) are endorsed and liberal institutions in place, they "tend to encourage the cooperative virtues of political life: the virtue of reasonableness and a sense of fairness, a spirit of compromise and a readiness to meet others halfway, all of which are connected with the willingness to cooperate with others on political terms that everyone can publicly accept."[66] In short, the viability and attractiveness of liberal principles and institutions tends to affect the ways in which people think about them at the domestic level.

These principles are perhaps more likely to be comprehensible and attractive in societies very different from the ones in which they were first formulated than their critics might suppose. "When Rawls's *Theory of Justice* was translated into Chinese it served not only to further academic study of the west but also to provide a resource for civil libertarians looking to reform China's political structure. Its alleged Anglo-American biases in accounting for human nature were no obstacle to its use—suggesting that such biases were insignificant."[67]

Rawls hypothesizes that, over time, variants of previously non-liberal comprehensive doctrines capable of providing appropriate support for an overlapping consensus endorsing political liberalism might emerge.[68] In turn, the need to justify their views to others who cannot simply be ignored or silenced would require people to rethink their comprehensive doctrines and to recast their grounds and implications in light of their new political environment. They would seek to explain their underlying convictions and the specific policy recommendations following from these convictions in ways at least comprehensible to those who did not share their comprehensive doctrines.[69] (Doing so would be especially challenging because of the need to articulate responses to a wide range of diverse issues.[70]) As with an overlapping consensus developed over time, citizens would come authentically to endorse political liberalism not merely out of expediency but as an expression of their own underlying convictions.

There is no reason a consensus of this sort could not emerge at the global level. The same kinds of pressures that might incline proponents of diverse views to support liberal institutions once they were in place domestically could generate support for such institutions globally. The inherent attractiveness of such institutions could become apparent once people became accustomed to them and were in a position to compare them with alternatives. Even were people not liberally inclined initially, they might change their minds once given the opportunity to live as equal persons within free institutions.

Again, there is no way of determining for certain whether an overlapping consensus in support of a liberal global regime would develop. However, the same factors that might make the cosmopolitan liberal hope that a consensus in support of a regime already existed, together with the considerations to which Rawls points in support of his contention that such a consensus could develop at the domestic level, might make the cosmopolitan's expectation that such a consensus might emerge globally appear less naïve.

One factor that might help to foster an emergent consensus in favor of cosmopolitan liberal principles is the potential link between nonliberals' comprehensive doctrines and the principles endorsed by cosmopolitan liberals. It is obvious that the principles that make up justice as fairness are controversial and will continue to be so for the foreseeable future.[71] Rawls nonetheless regards these principles as capable of earning the support of a domestic political consensus. In part, this is perhaps best seen as a consequence of understanding these principles as derived by implication from convictions widely shared in liberal political cultures. Rawls appears to believe that, if taken seriously, the basic norms of equality, freedom, and fairness to which people in such cultures assent entail support for something like his two principles of justice—even if the implications of these basic norms have not previously been evident.

Stable support for these principles might follow, then, from citizens' recognition that to endorse common standards of equality, freedom, and fairness is therefore also to endorse something like a Rawlsian understanding of justice. Perhaps the same might be true globally: while a number of peoples might initially be inclined to reject the specific principles contained in a Law of Persons, they might ultimately come to see the acceptance of these principles as inescapable because they appear, perhaps surprisingly, to follow from more general, abstract norms they already endorse.[72]

It is also worth emphasizing that the process of forging a global consensus in favor of a cosmopolitan account of global justice can be fostered by clear choices on the part of people in liberal societies. Respecting the freedom of others to trade and move freely throughout the globe and avoiding military and political interference with other societies can help to foster greater interchange and the emergence of increased consensus on liberal values. A consensus on the basis of which a cosmopolitan account of global justice could be constructed may thus be seen as a goal to be achieved rather than as an existing state of affairs constraining the pursuit of global justice.

### 4. A Law of Persons Might Acquire Legitimacy in Virtue of Its Endorsement by People Employing Liberal Norms of Public Reason

A cosmopolitan liberal could argue that a Law of Persons would enjoy Rawlsian legitimacy were it endorsed by persons committed to Rawlsian norms of (domestic) public reason. She could go on to note that such norms, themselves grounded in the deliberations of parties in the original position,[73] require commitment to freedom and equality and exclude comprehensive doctrines, even reasonable ones, from the public political realm. She might observe that proponents of nonliberal positions could not defend their positions using Rawlsian (domestic) public reason. She might conclude, therefore, that, if the kind of justification required for Rawlsian legitimacy is justification using Rawlsian (domestic) public reason, a liberal conception of justice could achieve global public justification in roughly the same way that a politically liberal view could achieve domestic public justification.[74]

This need not be a merely definitional victory. The cosmopolitan liberal could offer substantive reasons for her position. She could argue that she is perfectly prepared to defend a global version of political liberalism: she is not simply ruling those who disagree with her out of court. She could argue hypothetically using comprehensive doctrines she does not share if doing so makes her position comprehensible and persuasive to persons with nonliberal views.

Most fundamentally, however, the cosmopolitan liberal could note that the idea of free public reason *is itself a liberal notion*. Because it depends on the assumption that persons are free and equal, the idea of free public reason cannot effectively be invoked in support of fundamentally nonliberal positions. It requires accountability to all persons as reasonable decision makers and deliberately excludes certain kinds of reasons from consideration. A nonliberal, then, cannot simply invoke this principle to reject a liberal position.

Of course, we shouldn't assume that all liberals are cosmopolitans. But a noncosmopolitan liberal, Rawlsian or otherwise, would have difficulty invoking liberal public reason at the global level to argue against the fundamental moral and political equality of persons at the global level, though of course she would invoke public reason to argue that, as a matter of fact, cosmopolitanism would have difficulties in generating an overlapping consensus, for instance.[75]

The canons of public reason constrain the outcome of public debate in ways that seem likely to require broadly liberal conclusions. And the principle of legitimacy itself requires justification in terms of public reason, so that the nonliberal must either accept justification in terms of public reason—in which case a liberal conception of justice will likely achieve public justification—or else ask for some other sort of justification. But a liberal's failure to justify an institution or policy in terms other than those acceptable as part of public reason need be no bar to legitimacy from the standpoint of individual deliberators in the second original position. On its own terms, therefore, a liberal conception of global justice could be publicly justified. (The liberal could also, of course, seek to defend global cosmopolitanism, not with reference to an overlapping consensus of the sort Rawls's later work sees as essential at the domestic level, but rather in terms of the basic moral considerations, however grounded, to which he appeals in *A Theory of Justice*. She could argue that the success of arguments drawing on these considerations could show that a Law of Persons defended along the same lines as Rawls's initial account of domestic justice was satisfactorily warranted. This obviously wouldn't qualify as public justification of the sort Rawls seeks in his later work, though it would presumably offer liberals of some varieties sufficient reason to regard cosmopolitan justice as legitimate.)

It would obviously be open to a nonliberal to respond by challenging a global application of political liberalism in general. It is, of course, entirely possible that she might be right: there is no guarantee that political liberalism is the most reasonable political theory. What she could not do, however, is to challenge it by maintaining that it lacked Rawlsian public justification secured using domestic-style Rawlsian public reason. At best, a continuing challenge to a global political liberalism would undermine the ability of cosmopolitan liberals to bring into being a global legal regime marked by a desirable level and kind of stability. It would not prevent a Law of Persons from achieving Rawlsian public justification, because nonliberal views cannot be defended using public reason as Rawls's has defined it at the domestic level.

A complicating factor: Rawls evidently views *global* public reason as subject to constraints different from those that apply to domestic public reason. The norms of public reason operative in the Society of Peoples are those "appropriate to the Society of Peoples."[76] And because representatives of peoples rather than persons frame Rawls's Law of Peoples, it is to peoples—often governed by persons committed to nonliberal comprehensive doctrines—that public justification will be owed.

Rawlsian deliberators at the global level would frame a Law of Peoples that required that public justification be offered to *peoples* in ways that respected their freedom and equality. The norms of public justification they would adopt would thus not exclude the claims of nonliberal societies from consideration. But this is a consequence of Rawlsian ground rules for the formulation of the Law of Peoples, and so it cannot be used to rule out alternatives absent arguments in support of those ground rules.

Once it is clear that peoples should be treated as foundational when principles of global justice are being formulated, there is a credible case for the use at legal and related debates at the global level of arguments constrained by canons of public reason respectful of the diverse comprehensive doctrines endorsed in well-ordered societies. But if the question is whether peoples *should* be treated as foundational in the first place, these sorts of canons can't be invoked to show that they should. *Individual* deliberators would be warranted in opting for norms of public reason that govern domestic public life in a society that would count as just in relatively Rawlsian terms (presuming they would constrain public reason at all in the way Rawls's later work suggests they would), and whether a Rawlsian account of global justice understood as formulated by individual deliberators is appropriate or not will need to be settled by evaluating the relevant arguments, not by ruling out cosmopolitanism in advance through an appeal to a constrained conception of public reason.

Another sort of public reason argument against a cosmopolitan ground for global justice might focus on the exclusion of comprehensive doctrines from a foundational role in settling questions of justice. "There is no reason," Rawls says in respect of domestic justice, "why any citizen . . . should have the right to use state power to decide constitutional essentials as that person's . . . comprehensive doctrine directs. When equally represented, no citizen could grant to another person . . . that political authority. Any such authority is, therefore, without grounds in public reason."[77] He seems to want to make a similar move on the global level. It's as if he were to say: "There is no reason why any people should have the right to use *its* power to decide constitutional essentials for another people as its own comprehensive doctrine directs. When equally represented, no people could grant to another people that political authority. Any such authority is, therefore, without grounds in public reason." But the idea of this kind of application of Rawlsian principles of public reason to the global sphere seems unattractive.

The endorsement of cosmopolitan norms of global justice by liberals need not involve the imposition of a *comprehensive doctrine* by these peoples on others. If they embraced Rawls's turn to public reason, liberals peacefully promoting liberal values could do so on the basis of a purely *political* conception of justice, not a comprehensive doctrine.

In addition, the objection *presupposes* that peoples should be treated as equal. It is hardly surprising that equal peoples would endorse canons of global public reason that would rule out fundamental challenges to at least some nonliberal cultural, legal, and political regimes. Equal *persons*, however, would not.[78] They would be much more likely to adopt global norms—whether substantive or procedural—that respected their equality. Rawlsian domestic norms of public reason obviate justification of societal institutions, practices, and norms in terms of unreasonable comprehensive doctrines. The adoption of similar norms at the global level would rule out fundamentally nonliberal objections to the cosmopolitanism. Only those positions prepared to argue in publicly defensible ways would count, and since only disagreements couched in terms of Rawlsian public reason would *count*, there would be no real question about the legitimacy of a global regime committed to liberal norms of justice.

5. *The Justification of a Law of Persons Is Reasonably Conceivable*
It might be thought that a cosmopolitan norm of global justice, a Law of Persons, would be unable to achieve public justification. But a cosmopolitan could defend the possibility that such a Law could be publicly justified along multiple lines. She might suggest that existing comprehensive doctrines provided significant support for cosmopolitanism. She might tell a plausible story about the emergence over time of public justification for a Law of Persons parallel to the story Rawls tells about the emergence of domestic justification for justice as fairness. And she might envision the use of liberal norms of public reason to rule out opposition to cosmopolitanism from counting against the public justification of a Law of Persons. She could thus be warranted in regarding public justification for such a Law as a viable possibility.

**E. Rawlsian Constructivism Need Not Be Seen as Justifying the Rejection of Cosmopolitanism**
*1. Rawls's Constructivism Does Not Give Us Good Reason to Reject Cosmopolitanism*
Rawls's later turn to constructivism might be seen as offering support for his people-based starting point and for undermining the plausibility of the claim that public justification might be available for a Law of Persons.[79] His constructivist approach emphasizes building on existing social practices and assumptions (Subsection 2). Perhaps current international law might be seen as more cosmopolitan than Rawls's approach suggests, and this might offer partial constructivist grounding for a Law of Persons (Subsection 3), though international law shouldn't be seen as the only source of the elements to be used in constructing a Law of Persons or generating support for it (Subsection 4). But it may also be important to question whether support based on an overlapping consensus should be seen as essential (Subsection 5) and, indeed, whether the constructivist approach itself is inordinately relevant to the status

of the Law of Peoples (Subsection 6). The constructivist challenge shouldn't be seen as ruling out cosmopolitanism (Subsection 7).

## 2. Rawlsian Constructivism Builds on Existing Institutions and Norms

Rawls may be seen as unconcerned in *The Law of Peoples* with crafting standards for global justice drawing on or formulating first principles.[80] On this view, he simply begins with the existing practice of international relations and seeks to articulate principles for its improvement—to foster peace and fair cooperation between societies.[81] He seeks to build his account of global justice on the foundation of current international legal practice, which does, in fact, treat states as fundamental. Thus, peoples are represented in his second original position on essentially pragmatic grounds—because states are, in fact, central players on the contemporary global stage.

Rawls's approach might make sense as part of a constructivist project of justification for at least two distinct reasons: (*i*) commitments to extant international law norms imply a commitment to the principles expressed in those norms, so that putative requirements of justice flowing from those principles can be seen to be justifiable to many political actors in existing societies because the principles themselves are already embraced by those actors, and (*ii*) the fact that many societies are already committed to these principles might be expected to render support for requirements flowing from them more stable. Rawls's proposed global original position validates "principles that we already believe to be very important."[82] By contrast, there is no global consensus supportive of the essential moral equality of persons, so requirements of justice embodying belief in this sort of equality would be hard to treat as justified and would likely prove unstable.

## 3. A More Optimistic View of Current International Law Might Ground a Positive Response to the Constructivist Objection

A defender of cosmopolitanism could argue in response that existing international law norms do, in fact, increasingly seem to embody a fundamental principle in accordance with which individual persons deserve to be treated as having claims independent of those of states. This certainly seems to be the case as regards the emerging international human rights regime. While support for this regime is doubtless not as robust as support for some other features of the existing international legal system—with which, indeed, it would seem to be in tension—there is, indeed, *some* significant existing support for it (if there weren't, it would presumably collapse into irrelevance). And this might be thought to yield a measure of stability to norms of justice reflecting a principle embodied in the international human rights regime.

To be sure, the existing international legal regime is not primarily concerned with individual persons' relationships but rather with states' relationships with one another and individuals' relationships with particular states. However, this doesn't mean that the existing international order provides no basis for the elaboration of a more individually focused account of justice. The fact that particular persons are understood to have claims against particular states— not just for gross human rights abuses but also, at any rate when the states consent, for tort and contract violations—underscores the independent international status increasingly enjoyed by individuals, as does the possibility of criminal liability, by means of "universal jurisdiction," for serious human rights violations. And of course international commercial law does, indeed, facilitate relationships and enforceable commitments involving identifiable individuals. This is not to claim, of course, that the existing international legal order is focused primarily on individuals or that it accords them, rather than states, foundational status, but only that the increasing recognition of their independent significance might be seen as contributing to a trajectory of growing support for the kind of understanding required to ground a cosmopolitan account of justice.

*4. Legal Resources Need Not Be the Only Bases on Which a Law of Persons Could Be Constructed*
At the domestic level, Rawls envisions his constructivist procedure as operating on raw materials provided by various elements extant in political culture. These presumably include various moral and political traditions, and perhaps other supporting features of public discourse. The same ought to be true at the global level: existing

human rights norms and other features of international law are relevant, but of course a Law of Persons (like a Rawlsian Law of Peoples) need not be envisioned as emerging directly from these foundations. What matters is the existence of attitudes and convictions likely to ground proposed norms of global justice. These attitudes and convictions may reflect the influence of, say, international legal norms; but they might also have other sources.

Thus, contributions to global political culture would be important—moral arguments, including Rawls's own, might play a particularly significant role. Ideas and institutions created for the purpose of fostering commercial interaction will make a difference. So will literature, film, television programming, music, and other media products that serve in various ways to promote cooperation and encourage people to embrace egalitarian views of human rights and social status. All these can provide materials from which a global order conducive to support for a Law of Persons could be constructed and from which the key elements of such a Law could be derived. Of course a Law of Persons wouldn't necessarily be a simple transcription of elements in existing texts, but it could reasonably be seen as building on them.

*5. It May Be Worth Questioning the Significance of a Global Consensus in Support of Particular Norms of Justice*
Defenders of the potential viability of cosmopolitanism can point to tendencies in current international law, particularly human rights law, that seem to reflect significant, and perhaps growing, regard for individual persons rather than states. The existence of such tendencies can be seen as reason to believe that a Law of Persons could come to be seen as legitimate and to acquire the support needed to qualify as stable. But despite these tendencies, it is doubtless correct that the existing international law regime as a whole (human rights law, which is not itself uniformly concerned with particular persons, may be an outlier) is overwhelmingly statist.

Defenders of Rawls's people-based approach can obviously maintain that "we already believe" that existing principles of international law that affirm the equality and foundational role of states should be seen as "very important." There will, of course, be some dispute about whether "we" take this position or whether it is simply widely shared among those who embrace the current international status (statist?) quo, which might not be endorsed by those disadvantaged by the extant global order. The appeal to consensus in this context seems to serve primarily (whether or not that is why it is supported, by Rawls or by his defenders) to dramatically narrow the range of acceptable principles of global justice.

Defenders of Rawlsian legitimacy and stability may sometimes be confusing the articulation of principles of global *justice* on the one hand with the development of currently viable principles of international law on the other. It might well be, for one reason or another, that the implementation of this or that principle of justice might prove incapable of being implemented—though international human rights law may be seen as offering some reason for optimism regarding the prospects for a Law of Persons. But that's different from supposing that the principle isn't a principle of justice.

Thus, for instance, consider Leif Wenar's defense of his position that a cosmopolitan account of global justice should expect to incorporate existing international law norms. Wenar seems to me to assume much too blithely that existing political and legal norms are consistent with the requirements of justice. He maintains that "[w]e do not believe that American soldiers violated the basic rights of those Iraqi individuals" whom they killed during the first Gulf War and that "[t]he American soldiers were not murderers, even though the Iraqi individuals who were killed were not (before the American invasion) threatening the Americans' lives, or anyone else's lives for that matter." Wenar supposes that we should somehow see ourselves as committed to the view that people may "kill and be killed for the sake of protecting [states'] territorial integrity."[83] If beginning from a putative global consensus is a desideratum of what Wenar regards as a plausible account of global justice, we would, I think, be better off abandoning Wenarian plausibility. A cosmopolitan account of justice is attractive precisely because it provides us with a vantage point from which we can critically assess the bromides offered by the defenders of war and empire. And we ought to be critical of any account to the extent that it fails to do so. (There will be reason, on cosmopolitan Rawlsian grounds, to criticize such accounts, but of course that's not an argument *for* cosmopolitanism. However, if cosmopolitanism fits, as I believe it does, more snugly with egalitarian liberal moral intuitions than does statism, that will be a reason at least to look doubtfully on statist positions like Wenar's.)

## 6. The Relevance of the Constructivist Approach Itself Could Reasonably Be Questioned

The understanding of the Law of Peoples elaborated in Rawls's 1994 lecture on the topic and again in *The Law of Peoples* doesn't differ significantly from the version articulated in *A Theory of Justice*. There is little reason to think that the constructivist approach adopted after *Theory* played any central role in the formation of Rawls's thinking about the nature and justification of the Law of Peoples, even if he came to see his constructivism as providing a path to elaborating an account of global justice he had earlier been inclined to defend in different terms. While a constructivist justification for the Law of Peoples may be available, it is unlikely to be closely related to Rawls's own motivations.

## 7. Cosmopolitanism Can Be Affirmed in the Face of a Challenge Rooted in Rawlsian Constructivism

A constructivist method for doing political philosophy could be thought to help ground a people-based approach to global justice and to pose difficulties for a person-based one, but constructivism need not have this implication. To be sure, Rawlsian constructivism does begin with exiting institutions and beliefs. But these need not be seen as being resolutely statist. And existing currents in global culture and political morality may provide resources for the elaboration of a Law of Persons even if current international law norms offer insufficient grounding for such a Law. There is, I think, considerably more to recommend the Rawlsianism of *Theory*, in which liberalism is defended as a comprehensive doctrine, than the Rawlsianism of the later Rawls. But I don't think constructivism need be seen as an insurmountable barrier to the adoption of a Law of Persons, for the sorts of reasons I have already suggested. Resources on the basis of which a liberal account of global justice could be constructed are available at the global level. Constructivism need not undermine liberal cosmopolitanism.

## F. A Law of Persons Could Achieve Legitimacy without Consensus

*1. Legitimacy Need Not Depend on the Occurrence of Consensus*
A Law of Persons might be publicly justified, but the public justification of a principle of political morality should not be seen as required for it to bind persons and institutions. Our understanding of public justification itself should be sufficiently nuanced to make clear that this kind of justification needn't involve unanimity (Subsection 2). Stability for the right reasons could emerge globally in much the same way as it could emerge at the domestic level (Subsection 3), though stability need not be a precondition for legitimacy (Subsection 4), particularly given that significant moral duties clearly don't depend on the occurrence of stability (Subsection 5). A Law of Persons could qualify as legitimate (Subsection 6).

*2. Public Justification Need Not Be Seen as Requiring Unanimity*
Perhaps a political conception is publicly justified in a given society only if everyone in the society endorses it. It would seem, then, that the Law of Peoples could be legitimate, that it could bind the world's people, that global institutions could act in accordance with its terms, and that, absent such a government, smaller-scale social institutions of the relevant sort could be bound by it and could demand that others conform to it—but only if all the world's people had assented to it.

And, indeed, Rawls sometimes appears to suggest that public justification requires unanimity.[84] But Rawls does not say that all citizens must *in fact* endorse a political conception for it to count as justified. Rather, he suggests that in a well-ordered society, the terms of cooperation are set on the basis of what "all *can* endorse as just."[85] It is one thing to say that everyone *can* reasonably endorse political liberalism and quite another to say that a politically liberal regime is just only if everyone *does*, in fact, endorse the basic principles that ground it.

Rawls clearly recognizes that, while all those adhering to the canons of public reason might be able to affirm political liberalism and either justice as fairness or some nearby view, not everyone would endorse these canons. "Views that would suppress altogether the basic rights and liberties affirmed in the political conception [governing a politically liberal society], or suppress them in part, say[,] its liberty of conscience, may indeed exist, as there will always be such views."[86] Rawls simply holds out the hope that "they may not be strong enough to undermine the substantive justice of the regime."[87]

*3. Global Stability Could Be Achieved in the Same Manner and to the Same Degree as Domestic Stability*
At the domestic level, the kind of support Rawls envisions for a stable political order does not seem to be primarily the work of a powerful state enforcing agreement on rules. While he clearly does support the existence and operation of such a state, overlapping consensus provides support for the account of justice underlying state enforcement activity, so state activity cannot be appealed to as the *source* of that consensus. And it is clear empirically that multiple sources distinct from state activity contribute to the shape of liberal political morality.

A Rawlsian critic of cosmopolitanism could, of course, maintain that whether an account of justice is domestically justified is a contingent matter, ultimately dependent on the emergence of a domestic overlapping consensus, something that can't be guaranteed in advance. But to the extent that an account of justice *can be* justified domestically despite considerable disagreement, it would seem that widespread cross-societal disagreement need not undermine the justification of a Law of Persons.

*4. Legitimacy Could Obtain in the Absence of Proper Stability*
If a supporting consensus didn't exist, justice as fairness would be "in difficulty";[88] it might even be the case that no liberal position could attract stable support.[89] And Rawls (surely rightly) regards this possibility as troubling. But he does not suggest that it would call into question the actual reasonableness of justice as fairness. Lack of

a stable overlapping consensus in support of a Law of Persons need not call the *legitimacy* of such a Law into question. A global government would not be needed to implement it; absent such a government, individual legal systems and other institutions could still be bound by it and could still demand that others adhere to it. Even if a Law of Persons had not yet achieved public justification, none of the responsibilities or rights flowing from such a Law—at least, none with which I am concerned here—need be impaired.

*5. Robust Duties May Obtain Independent of Consensus-Based Support*

Rawls explicitly grants that peoples have responsibilities and rights with respect to other societies that have not, it appears, acknowledged the legitimacy of the Law of Peoples. They have the responsibility to aid "burdened societies"[90] and to respect the rights of individual combatants and noncombatants in war.[91] They have the right to defend themselves and others against attacks by "outlaw states."[92] They also have the right—and perhaps the duty—to exert pressure on outlaw states to end human rights abuses.[93] He evidently believes, then, that liberals may be bound by the Law of Peoples whether or not at least some nonliberal societies endorse it. At best, then, a consensus of liberal (and perhaps decent nonliberal) peoples might be regarded as needed to sustain a Rawlsian Law of Peoples. A society need not embrace such a consensus, however, in order to be treated as bound by the Law of Peoples (an outcome largely guaranteed by the definition of liberal and decent nonliberal peoples).

It must be possible, therefore, for the Law of Peoples to be legitimate and binding even if a significant number of peoples resist accepting it. And if this is so, a Law of Persons could be binding, too, even if there were significant disagreement with its requirements (even as, presumably, it was endorsed by a consensus of cosmopolitan liberals—defined, as in Rawls's global account of the original position, in such a way that they might be expected to embrace it). Whether under a Rawlsian Law of Peoples or a Law of Persons, societies would be seen as bound by at least some requirements of justice they had not acknowledged as legitimate. On Rawls's own view, well-ordered societies would be required to abide by the Law of Peoples whether or not it was globally publicly justified, even when dealing with peoples and persons who failed to accept its validity; the same would be true, *mutatis mutandis*, of a Law of Persons.

Rawls seems prepared implicitly to acknowledge that at least some norms intended to be global in scope can be appropriate and binding even if not publicly justified (or even if justified only with respect to a significantly narrowed public). Rawlsian duties of aid and duties in war, for instance, obtain without anything like global public justification. Given that such justification does not appear to be essential to the binding character of duties Rawls himself recognizes, it would seem difficult to ground a critique of cosmopolitanism successfully in the requirement of public justification.

*6. Even without a Definitive Overlapping Consensus Supporting It, a Law of Persons Might Reasonably Be Regarded as Legitimate*

We should not suppose that a Law of Persons would lack legitimacy until supported by an overlapping consensus of reasonable comprehensive doctrines. Such a Law could be authoritative whether or not it had achieved public justification, just like various serious moral duties. It might, of course, *be* publicly justified, even if not unanimously endorsed. And it might exhibit stability for the right reasons for the same reasons Rawlsians might think justice as fairness might do so at the domestic level. Thus, a Law of Persons could be reasonably regarded as legitimate.

## G. A Law of Persons Could Be Legitimate and Adequately Justified

Even in the face of at least some Rawlsian strictures on justification, a Law of Persons could nonetheless prove legitimate. A supporting overlapping consensus of reasonable comprehensive doctrines in support of a Law of Persons might already exist; and, if it does not, it might emerge simply because of the attractiveness of liberal ideals and their widespread influence. If Rawlsian limits on public justification were applied at the global as well as the domestic level, so that only reasonable comprehensive doctrines accepting the canons of Rawlsian public reason needed to be taken into account, the likelihood that a Law of Persons could achieve Rawlsian legitimacy would obviously be even greater. And Rawls's constructivist approach to doing political philosophy needn't be seen as grounding a successful challenge to the legitimacy of a Law of Persons. In addition, there is good reason to think that the validity of (at least) some aspects of political morality should not be seen, even by Rawlsians, as depending on their legitimacy, and therefore on their public justification. While specific policies and institutional arrangements might lack binding force absent legitimacy, basic principles of justice, at any rate, evidently do not. Rawlsians are not bound by Rawls's own views, of course, but his own treatment of issues including war and cross-societal aid suggests that the demands of justice apply whether or not these demands have been publicly justified on a global scale and whether or not those affected acknowledge them. It does not appear, then, that a Rawlsian argument focusing on public justification could effectively undermine the legitimacy of a Law of Persons.

## IV. Peoples Are Not Essential Features of the Global Scene

### A. *Arguments for the View That Equality Is Rooted in State Membership Don't Preclude a Cosmopolitan Starting Point for Reflection on Global Justice*

An approach to global justice that declines to treat people as equal across the boundaries of peoples, and so rejects cosmopolitanism, cannot be justified on the basis that states are inescapable features of life in a world like ours. Territorial affiliation need not be seen as a definitive of people's rights (Section B). Sovereignty is not needed in order to make the question of justice a live one (Section C). States are not collective agents, and being a collective agent is not necessary to qualify as a site of justice (Section D). And cultural affinity needn't be seen as justifying the special treatment Rawls accords to peoples (Section E). Arguments for treating states as globally basic in ways that rule out cosmopolitan norms of justice don't seem successful (Section F).

### B. *States Are Not Inescapably Foundational*

Wenar argues that cosmopolitanism is unsustainable because of the inescapability of states.[94] Beginning from the assumption that a world state is undesirable, he goes on to suggest that, in the absence of such a state "territorial powers with armed forces that may permissibly protect territorial borders will be a permanent feature of the global order." If this is the case, "then individuals' basic rights and liberties cannot be fully specified without reference to those individuals' territorial affiliations," with the result that "[n]o complete set of pure cosmopolitan principles is possible."[95]

I believe that deterritorialized systems of order maintenance and dispute resolution are both conceivable and attractive, and they are likely to enjoy more legitimacy, on multiple grounds, than territorially monopolistic states. Even if we granted the viability and desirability of states, however, it would not follow that basic rights and liberties couldn't be specified in a cosmopolitan original position. These rights could be generic, territory independent, and need not be understood as relative to people's territorial affiliations (except, perhaps, as regards their participation in particular state decision-making processes—though their entitlement to do so could still be specified globally), though states might be among the entities responsible for implementing them. Cosmopolitan criteria for justice could be formulated without giving states pride of place and could rightly constrain the actions of states in a variety of ways.[96] States need not be seen as inescapable in any way fundamentally threatening to a cosmopolitan starting point for reflection on global justice.

### C. Sovereignty Is Not a Prerequisite for Justice

A more elaborate version of this sort of argument might stress the putatively essential role of sovereign power in making justice possible.[97] On such an account, justice might be seen as a precondition for what would otherwise be the arbitrary rule by a state over the people in a given territory. Absent the possibility of justice between them, it makes no sense, on this view, to talk about people as morally or politically equal.

State boundaries are, admittedly, quite contingent. But an entity exercising sovereign power within those boundaries simultaneously subjects those it rules to substantial coercive constraints and at least to some degree involves them in a common enterprise by claiming to rule in their name. The requirements of justice arise precisely because of this twofold state activity. An entity that exercises the relevant sort of coercive power, at least if its reach is relatively comprehensive, can reasonably do so only if it treats its subjects fairly—and so in accord with the requirements of justice. In turn, subjects are obligated to one another and to support the institutions of the state. State action that forms or sustains significant elements of the social infrastructure creates significant possibilities for coordination among subjects that would otherwise be unavailable. And their identification with the state, generated by its rule in their name, binds them in a common enterprise and gives them responsibility for the society-wide policies the state implements.

Thus, state actors have duties of justice because of the reach of their policies, the potential impact of those policies, and their use of coercion to implement those policies. State subjects have duties related to justice because the state rules in their name and because state action creates and maintains institutions that bring into being otherwise unsustainable cooperative possibilities. Once those institutions are in place, they can reasonably be expected to adhere to requirements of fairness, and citizens have a duty to support them.

For Rawls, requirements of justice are *institutional* requirements. They are not individual duties that obtain independently of actors' institutional contexts. Absent a global institution, or network of institutions, with the coercive power of a state, the issue of global justice simply doesn't arise. Duties in justice obtain *within* societies governed by states, not between them. Cosmopolitanism seems to assume that it is possible to talk about global justice with a focus on the rights and duties of particular persons, anterior to their membership in particular state-governed societies, even if it might be prepared to allow that such societies were derivatively valuable. But if talk about rights and duties in justice makes sense only within such societies, then the cosmopolitan starting point seems indefensible absent a global state, since it presupposes an unsustainable way of conceiving of justice. Equality in virtue of the two moral powers is rightly understood as equality only among persons jointly subject to state power.

An argument of this sort seems to carry some weight when the focus is specifically on Rawlsian *distributive* justice. On this view, a society is not simply a cooperative venture for mutual advantage, but a venture the terms of which are in significant part *created* by the exercise of state power. Because it sets the terms for cooperation among people in a given population, the state might well be seen to have an obligation to do so in a manner that treated them fairly. The fact that the state acts in the name of (at least some of) those it governs really adds little to the argument.[98] We can imagine a situation, for instance, in which a state exercises control over a given population but does so in the name of a smaller subset of that population (as, for instance, in the case of a slave society). In this case, the fact that the state identifies and enforces the legal rights of people in whose name it doesn't profess to act seems to create a problem that needs to be rectified as a matter of justice, rather than narrowing the scope of justice to those in whose name the state purports to act. Because slaves, say, possess the two moral powers, they are surely owed equal consideration in virtue of Rawlsian justice. Those in whose name the state purports to act might be thought to have particular duties to support its just acts, but they are not the only ones to whom Rawlsian domestic justice is owed. Those, at minimum, over whom the state exercises coercive power (and, it might be thought, thereby unites in a cooperative scheme—for there would be little reason, absent genocidal madness, to exercise coercive power over a population if its cooperation is not in some way to be sought) should be treated as equals for purposes of determining the demands of domestic justice.

It is easy to see why a sovereignty-based objection might be thought to apply to schemes calling for the global implementation of some Rawlsian domestic economic norms and policies. But Rawlsian justice as fairness isn't exclusively economic in nature, after all. The first principle of domestic justice protects the basic liberties. While these liberties constrain the operation of the second principle, they can be acknowledged and protected independently of it. They figure in a domestic account of justice because they serve as limitations on state power. But unlike *economic* justice as it is conceived in Rawls's official theory, they are not necessitated or occasioned by the need to distribute the product of a cooperative venture putatively created by state coercion.

It seems clear, then, that, whether or not it makes sense to talk about global distributive justice, it certainly could make sense to talk about global justice as involving the protection of the basic liberties. There would thus be something for individual deliberators in a global original position to do even if distributive justice were understood to be impossible absent a global sovereign. Sovereignty is not needed to make sense of talk about the basic liberties or of the requirement that they be respected. A global Law of Persons formulated by individual deliberators could be seen as defensible even if the sovereignty-based objection to global distributive justice proved entirely successful. And if it could be shown on Rawlsian grounds that the basic liberties ought to include basic rights to own and dispose of productive property and to migrate and trade freely,[99] the acknowledgment of the basic liberties at the global level could have considerable impact on the global distribution of wealth not only within but among societies.

As regards Rawlsian distributive justice at the global level, it seems important to distinguish the locus of the formulation of principles of justice from the locus of the enactment of these principles. One might accept the sovereignty-based argument as showing that duties with respect to the products of a cooperative venture created by the coercive action of a state are owed by the state (and, indirectly, its citizens) only to the participants in the venture. But it would not follow that the *content* of the principles governing those duties varied from society to society. Requirements of domestic justice might still, for all the sovereignty argument has shown, be appropriately formulated by individual deliberators in a global original position. And because it would include both requirements for Rawlsian distributive justice at the domestic level in tandem with the protection of basic economic liberties, a global Law of Persons could significantly constrain global wealth distribution.

It might be possible further to extend the scope of the requirements of justice formulated by individual deliberators at the global level without seriously questioning the sovereignty argument by stressing the significance of coercive action outside state borders. A state might well exercise sufficient coercive power, directly or indirectly, over people resident outside its territory to constrain their possibilities for cooperative interaction. And the extent of its involvement in their affairs might be such as to rise to demands of Rawlsian justice in a manner consistent with the sovereignty argument. It does not claim sovereignty over these territories, we may suppose, but its impact on them is great enough that duties of justice might well arise with respect to them.

Whether the sovereignty argument itself, even as nuanced, is finally persuasive is another matter. I believe it can be challenged by questioning its central assumption—that the operation of a sovereign state is a necessary condition for questions of justice to arise at the domestic level.

It is surely right that the existence and operation of a state would be a *sufficient* condition for such questions to arise. A state that coercively constrained and enabled people's cooperative activities in particular ways would surely have obligations related to its exercise of power (whether or not these would be just the obligations Rawls envisions). But it does not follow that such questions would not arise in a state's absence.

The notion that a state *would* be necessary for the question of distributive justice to be posed at the domestic level seems to be rooted in the assumption that the maintenance of social order requires the activity of a territorial monopolist. But there is in fact good reason to believe that people are quite capable of defining rights and duties and resolving disputes using bottom-up institutions that don't claim the monopolistic authority characteristic of states. A Hobbesian Leviathan isn't needed to prevent the war of all against all from taking place. On this model, no single, non-monopolistic domestic institution would obviously have the right or duty to oversee the contributions made by other institutions to the allocation of the wealth generated by cooperation in the society. But each institution could perfectly well be understood to be constrained by requirements of justice in its own operation. (And this is, of course, less different than might initially be supposed from what their proponents want and expect states to do, since states aren't unitary entities but in fact involve various associations, networks, and relationships of people who must all decide whether or not to act justly.)

To grant that this sort of approach to maintaining social order is viable at the domestic level, and could be constrained by requirements of justice formulated by Rawlsian domestic individual deliberators, is to grant, at the same time, that an analogue could be viable at the global level. A range of institutions—perhaps including states, perhaps not—at the global level could simply serve to maintain order and to respond to the requirements of justice. And those requirements could be understood to be those formulated by individual deliberators in a global original position.

The sovereignty argument doesn't rule out a cosmopolitan starting point for reflections on global justice in the absence of a world state. At most, the argument suggests limits on the scope of cosmopolitan justice: this kind of justice might be concerned with the basic liberties and with the requirements of domestic distributive justice without embodying requirements of global *distributive* justice. But the argument incorrectly assumes that state action is necessary for social order, and so for the question of justice to arise. If it is not, however, the question of global distributive justice can arise without the existence of a global state.

### D. *Putatively Shared Agency Doesn't Warrant the Treatment of Peoples as Foundational*

Philip Pettit has argued that Rawls's social ontology helps to explain and justify the priority he assigns to peoples at the global level.[100] Pettit argues that, if we understand the way in which Rawls implicitly conceives of a people as a collective agent, we will see both how Rawls seeks to ground his domestic account of justice and, at the same time, why he believes a global original position populated by representatives of peoples makes sense. On this view, people would be equal *as joint agents* rather than simply in virtue of their common humanity.

Pettit suggests that a people "organized for agency" will feature "continuous interaction between an exogenous representative government and an endogenously responsive citizenry. The members of any well-ordered people will be party to certain shared ideas that are capable of being articulated into a theory of justice. And they will control the government that represents them, they will constitute it as their representative, to the extent that the government is ordered or regulated by those common reasons, and by the corresponding conception of justice."[101]

A government organized in the manner Pettit describes will, he maintains, "be truly representative of the people," with the result that "the people will get to be established as an agent that is domestically and internationally effective."[102] At the domestic level, the members of a well-ordered people rely, and give one another reason to rely, on one another to behave in a manner reflective and respectful of the terms of their society's political structure and its underlying theory of justice—hence domestic political obligation.[103] And "[i]t is because they related to one another in the dense, structured manner of a well-ordered society that the members of a people owe so much to one another."[104] By contrast, global society features no such well-ordered structure—no institutions with shared agency.[105] However, "because well-ordered peoples are group agents, capable of performing like individual persons, . . . we can ask about how they related amongst themselves and about whether that mode of relationships supports any obligations of justice towards one another or towards less fortunate societies" and, in turn, why "we can think of such peoples being represented in a second original position."[106]

Pettit is clear that, on (his understanding of) Rawls's view, "it is a matter of stipulation that relevant relationships will be present amongst the members of any well-ordered society and absent across the membership of different well-ordered societies. That a society is well-ordered entails that the relationships will be present in the first case; that different well-ordered societies are distinct entails that they will be absent in the second."[107] A well-ordered society, then, is *by definition* one that is organized in such a way that it can function as a collective agent. It is thus simultaneously distinct from other societies *and* an appropriate subject of representation in a global original position.

The story Pettit envisions Rawls as telling is both elegant and impressive. But it is not obviously convincing. It does not feature a plausible account of collective agency (or obligation) at the domestic level. And if the account of peoples as collective agents at the domestic level proves unappealing, then it will not be available for use at the global level.

Pettit's Rawls imagines social cooperation as linking members of a well-ordered people at the domestic level in what he describes as a "dense structured manner"; he characterizes a well-ordered people as featuring "an intense, structured aspect."[108] As a general matter, however, I submit, our ties with our fellow citizens are relatively tenuous—whether measured in terms of the frequency of our contact with them, our emotional attachment to them and theirs to us, the degree to which they enter into our plans and we into theirs, or the degree to which we participate with them in any sort of deliberately conceived enterprise. Even the interactions among the residents of a small city don't exhibit much intensity.

Perhaps I am placing too much weight on Pettit's use of "dense" and "intense." But if we attend instead to his specific characterization of the dynamics of a society understood as a collective agent, we may find further reason to be skeptical. Interactions between citizens and governments are not continuous in any interesting sense. That is, citizens encounter state officials in a variety of capacities, but in the vast majority of cases they do so as customers—obtaining services from state agencies—or as subjects—submitting to the authority of state actors. Their interactions play no meaningful role in fostering accountability or ensuring that their intentions are expressed in the actions of state officials. They are unlikely to share anything like a robust theory of justice that consistently constrains and motivates state actors. And there is thus no meaningful sense in which they "control the government" or in which it "represents them." They exert little influence over it; they don't form or articulate or convey common reasons for state action; and, even if they do seek to influence state policies, neither they nor their putative representatives are characteristically guided by anything like a shared theory of justice.

States are not, in short, the sorts of collective agents Pettit's Rawls has in mind. So a plausible argument for a Rawlsian Law of Peoples cannot reasonably depend on an account like the one Pettit has offered. An account of domestic justice can perfectly well be rooted in moral requirements derived from a Rawlsian original position, or in some other manner, whether or not the citizens of a state form a collective agent, and the same could be true at the global level.

But suppose states were the relevant sorts of collective agents and their being so could serve as the basis for an account of domestic and global justice. Suppose, further, that collective agency of the sort Pettit has described were necessary to the occurrence of

Rawlsian justice. In such a case (however improbable), global cosmopolitanism might still prove defensible, because the citizens of a world state could form a collective agent. It doesn't seem as if size would be a decisive factor in making collective agency possible. If a small region can be a collective agent, so too can a large one—and so, I take it, a global one. A global state that possessed the same features that enabled collective agency at the regional level could exhibit collective agency.

Pettit's proposal for a Rawlsian social ontology is creative and provocative. But it doesn't seem to track our real-world experience of states, so it can't provide a basis for either domestic or global justice. And, even if it could, a world state could serve as a reasonable basis for cosmopolitan justice.

### E. Cultural Affinity among Their Members Wouldn't Warrant Treating Equality as Relevant Only within Peoples

A similar argument for a foundational role for peoples in Rawls's account of global justice might be rooted, not in the economic interconnections of the members of a particular people, but in their cultural ties.[109] While Rawls's position is often seen as a paradigmatic of modern liberalism, there is also, it may be argued, a communitarian side to his thought that has received less attention. His account of domestic justice may be seen as rooted in a robust sense of egalitarian community.[110] Similarly, his conception of peoplehood may be understood as rooted in a cultural affinity that determines the bounds of a society within which the requirements of domestic justice, and so the demand for equality among persons, should apply.[111]

Cultural affinity is obviously something many people value. And, though I am skeptical, it might well be seen as providing significant warrant for special obligations linking particular people. But the value of this sort of affinity could obviously be recognized by individual deliberators in a global original position. Its value would have to be understood as one among many preferences some people might have, so that just institutions would need to make room for its acknowledgment.

The proponent of a people-based account of global justice obviously needs more than this from the affinity argument. She needs,

I think, to maintain that there is good reason to regard the possession of the two moral powers as grounding moral and political equality among persons, and as generating requirements of justice, only in virtue of their participation in a common culture. (Such a view could, of course, leave room for less significant moral ties linking persons across the boundaries of peoples.) It seems to me, though, that cultural affinity can't ground the needed constraint on the moral reach of the essential equality of persons.

States generally lack cultural cohesion: their citizens embrace diverse individual projects, which they may see no reason to link with broader concerns affirmed by politicians and the culturally influential. There is no particular reason to expect that they will identify with the state as a prime source of identity. They also embrace diverse cultures and subcultures. Membership in these groups may be more important to their members than membership in a given state. At the same time, people may be linked to fellow participants in such cultural and subcultural groups across state-imposed boundaries. Migration can be expected to keep the cultural composition of a state's population in flux, and communication can be expected to present the members of that population with a wide range of possible identities and affinities that may connect them with others continents away. A modern state is unlikely to be a culturally cohesive project. And the attempt to make it one seems likely to fall foul of the demand for moral and political equality among members of a given society, which Rawls clearly sees as central to domestic justice in a liberal society.

The envisioned argument seems to be that the possession of the two moral powers renders people morally and politically equal within a society defined in virtue of its members' cultural affinity. But it seems unlikely that most, if any, modern societies could exhibit the needed sort of affinity. Someone who wants to affirm the significance of Rawlsian justice at the domestic level would thus seem required to acknowledge that affinity was of limited importance at best and so accept some sort of global cosmopolitanism or else to deny that Rawlsian justice has any immediate practical application even at the domestic level. To the extent that Rawlsians typically regard justice as fairness as currently applicable, the first option wouldn't be available to them.

Even in a world composed, improbably, of societies that happened to exhibit the relevant sort of cohesion, it is not clear that cultural affinity would justify treating a given society as a self-contained unit equal with other societies. Doing so might make sense if a society was made up of people who deliberately, voluntarily chose to participate in what they regarded as a collective enterprise. But if participation were involuntary, if dissent were repressed, and if the unconsenting were expelled, Rawlsian requirements of domestic justice would be violated. And it is difficult to see how a society could persistently maintain the needed sort of cohesion without violating those requirements. Only by ceasing to be a liberal society could a society come to exhibit the kinds of characteristics required, on the envisioned argument, for it to exhibit the needed sort of cohesion. Once it became a genuinely liberal society, the putative foundations of liberal justice would be lacking. Cultural cohesion seems an unlikely foundation for Rawlsian domestic justice. It will not be plausible on Rawlsian grounds to maintain that the two moral powers confer equality on people only if they are also participants in a common cultural enterprise.

## *F. Equality Needn't Be Understood as Obtaining Only within State Boundaries*

The kind of moral and political equality grounded in possession of the two moral powers can reasonably be understood as applying across the borders states seek to defend. A state-based conception of essential equality can't be persuasively defended on the basis that states are ineradicable features of life in a world like ours, that talk about justice only makes sense within the constraints created by a territorial monopolist, or that states should be treated as unified and rightly exclusive because of their putative status as joint agents or because of the cultural affinity supposedly linking their members. Equality may be affirmed as a characteristic of the relations of persons as such; it need not be seen as a function of membership in a particular state.

## V. Relativism Provides No Significant Support for Anticosmopolitanism

A Rawlsian relativist might argue that nonliberals would have no objective reason to endorse a Law of Persons. But Rawls himself is not a relativist.[112] And relativism provides, in any case, no support for an anticosmopolitan argument as such.

Rawls suggests that the principles of justice as fairness "are meant to answer the question: once we view a democratic society as a fair system of social cooperation between citizens regarded as free and equal, what principles are most appropriate to it? Alternatively: which principles are most appropriate for a democratic society that not only professes but wants to take seriously the idea that citizens are free and equal, and tries to realize that idea in its main institutions?"[113]

This might be understood as implying that his *argument as a whole* takes for granted the basic assumptions of freedom, equality, and democracy and then formalizes these assumptions in the original position. It might appear that he is simply interested in elaborating the implications of what "we here now" believe about these fundamental political issues.

This interpretation might seem to be suggested by Rawls's suggestion that "we look to the public political culture of a democratic society, and to the traditions of interpretation of its constitution and basic laws, for certain familiar ideas that can be worked up into a conception of political justice."[114] It might also appear to be supported by his assertions that "the principles of justice provide a response to the fundamental question of political philosophy *for a constitutional democratic regime*"[115] and that "the conception of the person is worked up from the way citizens are regarded in the public political culture of a democratic society."[116]

If this reading of Rawls were correct, the freedom and equality modeled in the first original position could only be defended in limited terms. Someone in a nonliberal society who did not view persons as free and equal would have no good reason to accept Rawls's domestic original position as aptly representing an appropriate starting point for thinking about domestic justice. (Such a person might also see no objective reason to accept a Rawlsian Law of Peoples, of course.) Of course, without more, this would not prevent liberals from acting on the assumption that such principles should guide the foreign policies of their societies.[117] They could certainly regard these principles as an appropriate expression of their sense of justice, to which on relativist grounds there could be no objection. They might argue that liberal principles are simply their "can't help[s],"[118] grounded in attitudes that they could regard on reflection as arbitrary but that are, as contingent matters of fact, deeply rooted in their cultures and in their psyches.[119]

But Rawls certainly does not talk, at least in general, as if he is a relativist. He affirms that "[p]olitical liberalism does not question that many political and moral judgments of certain specified kinds are *correct* and it views many of them as *reasonable*."[120] He supposes that "a liberal constitutional democracy is, in fact, superior to other forms of society."[121] He believes that nonliberal views of religious toleration are less reasonable than liberal alternatives.[122] His suggestions that we begin with the convictions central to liberal cultures when shaping an understanding of justice need not be read relativistically. Even if he treated the liberal principles of freedom and equality as given, as beyond criticism or demonstration, this on its own would not make him a relativist.

Indeed, he could simply claim (from within his preferred version of liberalism understood as a comprehensive doctrine, not as a political conception) that a liberal culture offers a more satisfactory route to a reasonable political morality than any other cultural environment and that he regards the assumptions that ground such a culture as accurate, even though he cannot, or at any rate does not seek to, demonstrate this in any compelling way.[123] On this sort of reading, one might say that the assumption of, for instance, equality, defended with the sorts of arguments offered in *A Theory of Justice* and *Justice as Fairness*, shapes the conditions obtaining within the first original position, but not that it is simply *presupposed* as an unquestionable given when those conditions are specified.[124] "[Just] because the exposition [of justice as fairness] begins with . . . [certain familiar ideas that can be worked up into a conception of political justice] does not mean that the argument for justice as fairness simply *assumes* them as a basis. Everything depends on how the exposition works out as a whole and whether the ideas and principles of this conception of justice, as well as its conclusions, *prove acceptable on due reflection.*"[125]

Focusing on "the leading conceptions of political justice found in our philosophical tradition" can be seen as a way of limiting the plethora of available options for reflection and selecting a convenient starting point, as well as identifying a viable basis for political consensus; it is not a relativistic assumption that the conviction that persons are free and equal is only "true for us" (whatever this might mean).[126] Our "can't help[s]"[127] and the assumptions dominant in our culture admit of criticism in the light of reason; they may, at least, turn out in some cases to be more than prejudices.[128]

Rawls must not suppose, then, that the assumption that persons are free and equal is simply a liberal *instinct*, even if it can't readily be defended using resources central to nonliberals' preferred comprehensive doctrines. It may well emerge from within liberal societies, and Rawls may regard himself as having in his later work justified it with reference to the political cultures of such societies. But he is certainly entitled to regard it as nonetheless more finally reasonable than the alternatives *in all societies*, whether or not explicitly acknowledged.

He evidently—and appropriately—regards his arguments for freedom and equality as reasonable and worthy of general endorsement (whether or not widely endorsed).[129] And his model of global justice is hardly relativist. Many human rights, even if not all those liberals believe important, are integral to the Law of Peoples as Rawls understands it.[130] Outlaw states are not allowed to behave as if their opposition to human rights and norms of global amity were true "for themselves," even if not for well-ordered societies.[131] And the views of decent nonliberal societies are taken into account in the first place—such societies are *regarded* by liberals as well ordered—precisely because of a prior moral assessment of their institutions and practices. Liberals are expected to judge that cooperation with decent nonliberals is not merely possible but also normatively appropriate.

In any case, in *A Theory of Justice*, at a point when he seems to have regarded his preferred understanding of liberalism as a comprehensive moral doctrine rooted in general, philosophically defensible moral principles, Rawls maintained that societies should be treated as equal for purposes of determining norms of global justice.[132] And this suggests that his later change of methodological course was not responsible for his embrace of a people-based approach to global justice.

Rawlsians need not be relativists. Rawls's own position isn't naturally read as relativist. If it were, Rawlsian relativism wouldn't necessitate tolerance for nonliberal regimes. And he had decided to treat peoples, rather than persons, as equal for purposes of formulating norms of global justice before any purported turn to relativism on his part took place. Relativism provides no basis for the rejection of cosmopolitanism.

## VI. Cosmopolitans May Reasonably Affirm the Global Equality of Persons

Rawls has suggested that *persons* should be treated as morally and politically equal at the domestic level because of their possession of the two moral powers. It seems appropriate to treat persons as morally and politically equal at the global level for the same reason. Rawls's explicit justifications for affirming the equality of peoples, and so the inequality of persons, at the global level are weak. But even the stronger arguments that might be offered against cosmopolitanism fail finally to persuade. In the absence of a stronger argument against the global equality of persons, it would seem sensible for liberals to accept Rawlsian considerations supporting the domestic equality of persons as entailing the equality of persons globally, too.[133]

Whatever Rawls's own reasons for opposing cosmopolitanism, defenders of a people-based approach could offer multiple reasons for accepting his preferred starting point. Cosmopolitans needn't show that Rawls's own position is internally inconsistent, but they can show that there are good reasons not to accept Rawlsian and related arguments against cosmopolitanism. A Law of Persons could qualify as legitimate. A global society grounded in such a Law could be a fair system of cooperation for mutual advantage, given a sufficiently nuanced and open-textured understanding of "system," and such a Law could bind even if it were not. It might achieve public justification, but it could be authoritative whether it did or not. The putative indispensability of states need not count against cosmopolitanism, not least because we shouldn't regard states as indispensable. There is no plausible relativist argument for preferring fairness to peoples over fairness to persons on the global stage—though Rawls's own views are not, in any case, relativist. There is good reason, in short, to retain a moral and political egalitarianism rooted in moral agents' possession of the two moral powers—and so to prefer a Law of Persons rather than a Law of Peoples.

Because it applied globally and because it defined the fundamental rights of particular persons whatever their circumstances, a Law of Persons would set the terms within which just institutions could operate at the local level. Judgments about justice and rights in particular societies would thus need to be formulated in its light. It would certainly be relevant, then, to relationships across societies, including those involving large-scale violence, and to the ways in which it would and would not be appropriate for liberals to tolerate nonliberal social and political institutions. In Chapter 4, I suggest that the core of a Law of Persons would be a set of cosmopolitan human rights—identical with those Rawls treats as basic at the domestic level (slightly elaborated to limit the use of force against noncombatants during violent conflicts), along with protections for productive property and global freedom of movement, as well as a general presumption of liberty—and I examine the limits such a Law might be expected to impose on violence and on liberal tolerance in a global order.

# CHAPTER 4

# Defining and Implementing a Law of Persons

## I. The Rights Protected by a Law of Persons Would Constrain Liberal Tolerance and the Use of Force

A cosmopolitan approach to global justice of the kind I have sought to begin elaborating here offers a distinctive perspective on human rights, toleration, and the use of force. The heart of a Law of Persons embraced by cosmopolitan deliberators would be a substantial array of human rights protections, including safeguards for "liberal" human rights—the Rawlsian equal basic liberties, several further guarantees, and a general presumption of liberty (Part II). These protections would likely impose more extensive limits on the use of force than Rawls's Law of Peoples (Part III). Thus, they would constrain the methods liberals could reasonably use to influence the behavior of nonliberals—precluding sanctions and military interventions—even as they also clearly limited liberal tolerance of nonliberal societies (Part IV). A Law of Persons would exhibit significant similarities with, but also significant differences from, a Rawlsian Law of Peoples (Part V).

## II. A Law of Persons Would Enshrine Robust Human Rights Protections

### A. *Cosmopolitan Deliberators Would Opt to Treat a Broader Range of Rights as Deserving Protection at the Global Level Than Would Rawlsian Deliberators*

Where Rawls's understanding of the human rights protections that would be incorporated in a Law of Peoples is significant but relatively narrow, a Law of Persons could be expected to safeguard a significantly broader range of rights. Liberal human rights of various sorts are conspicuously absent from the Law of Peoples, and, while it is possible to discern Rawls's likely motivations, they aren't altogether explicit (Section B). By contrast, the liberal rights, at minimum, that Rawls treats as central in his account of domestic justice would presumably be acknowledged by cosmopolitan deliberators, who could be expected to reason in the same way as their domestic counterparts (Section C). Cosmopolitan deliberators might well also see reason—as John Tomasi has suggested domestic Rawlsian deliberators should—to treat a number of economic liberties as basic, too (Section D). They might be inclined to incorporate explicit protections for freedom of trade and migration in a Law of Persons (Section E). More broadly still, cosmopolitan deliberators might opt for a variant of an approach taken by Rawls in early drafts of his account of domestic justice by embracing a very broad guarantee of liberty (Section F). A Law of Persons would safeguard more rights of more kinds than a Law of Peoples; it would be more consistently liberal, affording particular persons significant space within which to function as self-authors (Section G).

## B. Rawls's Law of Peoples Features Limited Human Rights Protections, for Which Rawls Offers Limited Explicit Justification

While a Rawlsian Law of Peoples would guarantee some human rights, the human rights protections it could be expected to feature would be limited.[1] For instance, full equality of citizens without respect to gender and religion would not be guaranteed under the Law of Peoples, there would be no assured right of democratic participation, and limits on freedom of expression would be acceptable.[2]

While Rawls describes the differences between the rights he believes should be protected by a Law of Peoples and the liberal human rights that would not be, he does little to justify the distinctions he makes. What warrants excluding "freedom of peaceful assembly and association"[3] while including "the right to own property alone as well as in association with others"?[4] (And why wouldn't ownership of property include the right to control what happens on that property—by, say, permitting an association to meet there or a public protest to take place there?) Why is "freedom of thought, conscience and religion"[5] protected, but not "freedom of opinion and expression"?[6]

Rawls's prime motivation in not safeguarding freedom of expression, association, and assembly, for instance, seems to be the articulation of a set of rights a nonliberal society could endorse. Instead of defining a well-ordered society as one that accepts a set of human rights justified on other grounds, Rawls may have chosen to identify the human rights protections contained in the Law of Peoples by asking, implicitly, what a decent nonliberal people could be expected to accept.

An obvious circularity problem looms, since what *makes* a decent nonliberal society *decent* is precisely its acceptance of these norms. Or put differently, the human rights protections that form part of the Law of Peoples will flow in part from the prior decision about which peoples to count as well ordered in the first place.[7] The norms Rawls is willing to treat as requirements for participation in the second original position seem to be identified in light of the logically prior judgment that societies that respect those norms should be included.[8] Counting as a well-ordered people means accepting the human rights norms that make up the Law of People; but a people qualifies for representation in a global original position for purposes of formulating such a Law only, it appears, in virtue of accepting previously stipulated human rights norms.

It seems relatively unlikely that global Rawlsian deliberators would treat a given norm as incorporated into the Law of Peoples unless acceptance of the norm has already been used to filter possible participants in a global original position. Such deliberators might thus be unlikely to adopt a complete list of human rights norms and corresponding interpretation more demanding than the least restrictive list or interpretation upheld by any of the peoples represented at the global level.

None of Rawls's global deliberators knows which society she represents, and none will know what her society's own preferred comprehensive doctrines or political circumstances are or what human rights guarantees each affords its members.[9] But it is not entirely clear whether participants *are* aware of the institutional arrangements that do obtain in various extant societies. It may be argued that treating them as possessing this kind of knowledge involves more specificity than Rawls is likely to want to allow, given his constraints on their counterparts at the domestic level. But *if* they do, none seems likely to opt for a version of the Law of Peoples that warrants affording more protection to human rights than is offered by the least protective of the participating peoples.[10]

Since the peoples are equal, none will be in a position to insist that another accept more rigorous human rights protections than it is already inclined to do. Each will need to consider the possibility that its human rights norms are the least protective of citizens and the least restrictive of officials of all those on offer. And if each participating society has adopted the level of human rights protection it offers *deliberately*, none will presumably want to accept higher standards, given that doing so would force it to act contrary to its considered preferences.

The human rights protections incorporated in a Rawlsian Law of Peoples are limited. Thus, even if they are open to such a Law, liberals will presumably not want to turn to it to determine which human rights are essential; instead, they will draw on their own preferred account of justice for the needed guidance. On this basis, they can proceed to determine which societies count as decent. Having done so, they could *then* judge to which form of the Law of Peoples Rawlsian deliberators would assent in a global original position. (They would not, of course, have to expect perfect compliance with any set of norms from either liberal or nonliberal societies.) But they could not determine these standards by means of a direct appeal to the contracting procedure underlying a Rawlsian Law of Peoples, without already identifying the peoples represented in a global original position.

Samuel Freeman defends Rawls's denial "that among the human rights must be included *liberal* freedoms of speech and association, with all that they include (for example, the right to defile or destroy national or sacred symbols, or enjoy pornography, or freedom of same-sex relations)." Freeman maintains that "[t]o hold otherwise is not to take the idea of human rights seriously."[11] Perhaps—but to hold otherwise seems to be to suppose that legal penalties for harmless sexual conduct could form part of a reasonable human rights regime. Given the serious legal penalties to which people are able to be subjected in multiple societies today because same-sex sexual relationships don't enjoy legal protection, this doesn't seem like a trivial matter. It is hard to imagine that cosmopolitan deliberators would regard legal regimes that permitted the use of force in response to people's consensual behavior as acceptable.

Of course, a great deal turns on what we mean, and on what Rawls means, by talking about and identifying human rights.[12] Enshrining human rights protections at the global level might be thought to play any of several different roles. They might be designed (*i*) to clarify what wrongs, if any, might reasonably trigger governments' just use of rectificatory or defensive military force or sanctions, (*ii*) to clarify what wrongs might trigger nonviolent pressure by one state on another, (*iii*) to spell out what wrongs, if any, might trigger the just rectificatory or defensive use of force by nonstate actors, (*iv*) to clarify what wrongs might trigger nonviolent pressure on a state by nonstate actors, (*v*) to clarify what societies should qualify as well ordered, (*vi*) to indicate which wrongs courts should be able to remedy *wherever* they occur (which ones qualify as subject to universal jurisdiction), (*vii*) to determine with what societies' liberal governments ought to enjoy diplomatic relations, or (*viii*) to clarify what protections any just legal system ought to feature, and so what limits on sovereignty are imposed by the requirements of justice. Each of these understandings of what global human rights protections amount to might be expected to offer a somewhat different account of which specific rights deserve recognition.

Rawls seems primarily interested in objectives (*i*) and (*ii*). Objective (*v*) needs to be met before a Rawlsian Law of Peoples can be formulated in the first place. It seems as if Rawls would want to affirm universal jurisdiction, per objective (*vi*), with regard to those rights he believes would be acknowledged by decent nonliberal peoples—with the understanding that the range of the relevant rights might be broader than the range of those rights appropriately triggering sanctions or military intervention, since universal jurisdiction as currently understood seems to involve primarily the imposition of legal liability on individuals rather than on regimes or governments.

Recognizing human rights doesn't seem designed, per se, to serve objective (*vii*) for Rawls, since he doesn't suggest, for instance, that well-ordered societies should necessarily deny diplomatic relations to benevolent absolutisms, for instance. And he doesn't seem particularly interested in objectives (*iii*), (*iv*), and (*viii*).

By contrast, many cosmopolitan liberals, I think, might be inclined to spell out their concern with human rights as a concern to realize objectives (*i*), (*ii*), (*vi*), and (*viii*). Objectives (*iii*) and (*iv*) are probably as (relatively) uninteresting to most cosmopolitan liberals as they are to Rawls. In *The Law of Peoples*, Rawls simply isn't interested in the question, *What rights do particular persons actually have?*, which many cosmopolitan liberals take themselves to be answering when talking about human rights. Instead, he wants to articulate and solidify a consensus among minimally decent regimes regarding the rights that ought to enjoy protection at the global level.

The broader question of what rights people actually have is, on my view, of continuing importance, and I think the answer should be much more expansive than Rawls's. And I am unsympathetic to the view that the active promotion of liberal rights should be constrained by the preferences of nonliberal governments. But there is a very real practical concern on Rawls's part that certainly deserves to be acknowledged and shared—a concern with placing practical limits on governments' use of military or equivalent force.[13] To the extent that we're focused on this concern, the constraints he suggests seem entirely reasonable—precisely, at least in part, because of the importance of the human rights that military action tends to violate. In particular, the notion that various positive rights can't be enforced by means of military intervention or sanctions is sensible and attractive—though of course military intervention isn't the primary means by which currently recognized human rights tend to be secured in any case.[14]

### C. A Law of Persons Would Include at Least the Liberal Human Rights Protections Rawls Acknowledges in His Theory of Domestic Justice

Individual deliberators might reasonably be less concerned than their Rawlsian counterparts about existing structures of power in nonliberal societies; concerned for themselves and those they represent, they would likely frame a Law of Persons that protected a range of human rights.[15] "Following the kind of reasoning familiar in the original position for the domestic case," such deliberators, as Rawls acknowledges, "would . . . adopt a first principle that all persons have equal basic rights and liberties," in a "way [that] would straightaway ground human rights in a political (moral) conception of liberal cosmopolitan justice."[16] If these rights were those that justice as fairness would safeguard at the domestic level, they would include at least "political liberty (the right to vote and to hold public office) and freedom of speech and assembly; liberty of conscience and freedom of thought; freedom of the person, which includes freedom from psychological oppression and physical assault and dismemberment (integrity of the person); the right to hold personal property and freedom from arbitrary arrest and seizure as defined by the concept of the rule of law."[17] In short, a Law of Persons would safeguard as wide a range of basic liberal human rights as those Rawls regards as likely to be enshrined in the constitution of a liberal state.

### D. A Law of Persons Might Treat Various Economic Liberties as Basic

#### 1. Economic Liberty Can Be Defended in Rawlsian Terms

Cosmopolitan deliberators would have good reason to agree with John Tomasi that some economic liberties should be treated as basic and so accorded lexical priority. Rawlsian justice as fairness does not offer fundamental safeguards for economic freedom (Subsection 2). Tomasi suggests some alterations in the Rawlsian framework that could ground such safeguards, defending them in terms Rawlsians might find appealing (Subsection 3). Tomasi's attractive defense of these alterations might be strengthened (Subsection 4), but his overall approach, both provocative and fruitful, points the way toward an intriguingly market-friendly Rawlsianism (Subsection 5).

## 2. Rawls's Preferred Approach Provides Relatively Narrow Protection for Economic Freedom and Seems to Encourage Ongoing Interference with Such Freedom

On Rawls's preferred account of the elements of justice, personal economic freedom doesn't seem to receive much *fundamental* protection. The basic liberties don't include protections for rights to own productive property and engage in market exchange.

Rawls's most recent account of the basic liberties safeguarded by his first principle of justice holds that these liberties are protected in virtue of their relationship to the two moral powers. Thus, they must be protected

1. in order "to ensure the opportunity for the free and informed application of the principles of justice to [the basic] structure and to its policies by means of the full and effective exercise of citizens' sense of justice";
2. in order "to ensure the opportunity for the free and informed exercise of [the capacity for a (complete) conception of the good] and its companion powers of practical reason and judgment"; or
3. because "they are necessary if the other basic liberties are to be properly guaranteed."[18]

On Rawls's own view, the right to own personal property is worth protecting in order to, among other things, "allow a sufficient material basis for personal independence and a sense of self-respect."[19] Thus, this right is defended with regard to its capacity to foster the realization of certain primary goods—it is not clear in which of the three categories he mentions Rawls sees it as grounded. Whether there ought to be a right to *productive* property is another matter, to be resolved politically. The same is true of other economic liberties.

The Difference Principle is said to be intended as a constraint on the "basic structure" of rights, institutions, and so forth, rather than as a guide for individual policy choices. But Rawls seems at points to see it as licensing substantial, ongoing interference with the distribution of wealth resulting from voluntary transactions.[20]

## Defining and Implementing a Law of Persons • 89

*3. Tomasi Proposes Limited but Significant Modifications to Rawls's Framework to Safeguard Economic Freedom for the Right Reasons*

Tomasi seeks to show that the essential shape of Rawls's theoretical approach to establishing the content of justice can be maintained even as it is modified to render it much more market friendly. I realize, of course, that Tomasi's proposals have been highly controversial among Rawlsians, and I do not intend to suggest that they are beyond question (or that similar conclusions couldn't be reached on alternative Rawlsian grounds). But I ask the reader to consider whether Tomasi's proposals might not, in fact, be attractive and plausible and to consider where they might lead.

Tomasi recognizes that Rawls does not see the basic liberties as forming an arbitrary laundry list. He argues that the Rawlsian rationales offered for affirming these liberties *as basic*, for defending rights to personal property and occupational choice, naturally lead, if taken seriously, to the recognition of a broader range of economic liberties as comparably basic. The bare choice of an occupation matters, of course, as an important means of shaping one's identity and identifying and articulating one's deepest concerns. But the same is true of other choices one makes related to work—with whom, under what conditions, and so forth. Restricting such choices amounts to a denial to people of opportunities to develop and exercise the two moral powers.[21]

The right to own *personal* property offers an important measure of autonomy, independence, and security; significant opportunities for self-expression; and support for one's identity. So too does the right to own *productive* property.[22] And the opportunities for participation in economic life provided by the opportunities to acquire productive property and to exchange personal and productive property (and, arguably, personal property *becomes* productive when exchanged) give people, as consumers and producers, multiple occasions for moral self-development and self-expression. Consumption has become a vital means of self-authorship for almost everyone in developed societies (and many in less-developed societies): people's life plans include consumption choices, and the identities they construct are signaled through various sorts of consumption. Thus, the economic liberties matter because they involve the freedom to acquire goods and services for consumption—but also the freedom to engage in the kind of productive economic activity needed to make consumption possible.[23]

Restrictions on economic liberties inhibit people's exercise of the two moral powers in substantial ways.[24] They also affect access to the primary goods Rawls sees as crucially important for all citizens. The ability to work productively and to see the worth of what one does validated by others is an important ground of self-respect. So is the recognition by one's peers of one's right (and so of one's potential capacity) to make one's own decisions about work, exchange, and care for their own needs.[25] Instrumental concerns related to the capacity of rights safeguarding work, exchange, and control over personal and productive property to maximize access to material goods and facilitate their efficient and responsive distribution also matter.[26] But Tomasi thinks Rawlsians should find the inescapability of the moral concerns reflected in these rights particularly compelling.[27]

Rights to use and exchange productive property and to make a wide range of occupational choices can be justifiably incorporated into the list of lexically prior basic liberties. The Difference Principle, too, can be reconceived. Maximizing economic freedom is, precisely, a way of implementing the Principle, because a genuinely freed market benefits the least-well-off class, the working poor, more than any realistically conceivable alternative.[28] A robust scheme of property rights and protections for exchange simultaneously makes the consumer goods that enrich the lives of everyone, including the working poor, more accessible and creates more opportunities for the working poor to improve their economic positions.[29]

*4. Additional Considerations Might Add Further Support to Tomasi's Case*

Tomasi labels his preferred approach *market democracy*. Market democracy simultaneously enshrines market freedom in the basic structure of society and justifies the protection of market freedom in virtue of its anticipated benefits to the least well off. The modifications to Rawlsian justice as fairness required to warrant market democracy on Rawlsian lines are finally worth embracing because market democracy is more inspiring, offering a more appealing conception of cooperative human life and personal self-development.

Tomasi's case for market democracy could arguably be strengthened in various ways. Even absent the reality of economic growth,[30] paternalism would have been questionable precisely because it impedes the self-authorship liberals rightly prize. And the deprivation early social-democratic theorists saw as warranting paternalism is best seen not as a consequence of market freedom but rather as an outgrowth of large-scale depredation, taking place over several centuries, and of ongoing efforts to privilege the wealthy and well connected. Similarly, one can perfectly well value democratic, human-scale workplaces while affirming that such workplaces can be fostered precisely not by mandating democratic structures but rather by eliminating the privileges that prop up hierarchies.

Even behind the veil of ignorance, basic economic and sociological knowledge is available. There are plausible arguments to the effect that liberal democratic socialism and Rawlsian property-owning democracy would generate incentives for political actors to engage in self-dealing mischief and for economic actors to reduce work and to seek political rather than economic success. In addition, the impossibility of replacing market calculation with top-down planning—both because of the inability of central planners to mobilize dispersed knowledge and because of the indispensability for economic calculation of markets in capital goods—render state socialism, even of a liberal-democratic variety, a nonstarter and pose serious problems for property-owning democracy. Thus, while market democracy might be seen as preferable to these social democratic alternatives because more inspiring, it should also be seen as superior to them in light of credible social-theoretic analysis.

*5. Tomasian Arguments for the Priority of Economic Liberty Embody Plausible Modifications of Rawls's Framework for Justice*
Tomasi attempts to demonstrate that the kinds of concerns that motivate Rawls's theoretical approach can find expression in an account of justice that offers robust protections for economic freedom. It's hard not to see this as a tour de force, given that Rawls's own approach doesn't feature such protections and might be seen as inhospitable to them. But Tomasi proposes changes to

Rawls's framework—changes that needn't be seen as either ad hoc or hostile to Rawls's project—that would leave that framework entirely recognizable while ensuring that it did, indeed, safeguard economic liberty. While additional considerations could perhaps add strength to Tomasi's arguments at some points, his defense of a market-friendly Rawlsianism as a variety of domestic justice is clearly strong and attractive on its own.

### E. Cosmopolitan Deliberators Would Have Good Reason to Incorporate Freedom of Trade and Migration in a Law of Persons

Allowing the free movement of people, goods, and services is simultaneously a matter of respect for the equality of persons, without regard to geographic origin or cultural identity, and a recognition of the welfare-conferring significance of liberating trade—for those on both ends of any trading relationship.[31]

Thus, a well-ordered people should decline to impose tariffs and erect other barriers to the entry and sale of goods from burdened societies while working with other societies to encourage the global adoption of a legal regime banning tariffs and similar restraints on exchange. There would be every reason to ensure that such a regime lacked the complexity and inconsistency of the existing set of rules negotiated under the umbrella of the World Trade Organization and that it instead involved simple nondiscrimination among societies and individual traders. At the same time, well-ordered peoples should ensure that no domestic policy barriers prevented their firms and citizens from investing productively in burdened societies.

Well-ordered peoples should also open their borders to allow untrammeled migration.[32] The foundational importance of occupational choice, the interests of individual migrants, the interests of those with whom they might seek to work in new locations, the interests of those benefiting from the remittances they might offer, and the interests of consumers of the goods and services they produced would all militate against the implementation of restrictions on immigration.

Gillian Brock criticizes the notion that immigration freedom should be seen as a panacea for problems in poor countries.[33] And she is surely right that other factors need to be addressed if the problem of global poverty is to be resolved satisfactorily. However, open immigration does contribute to the improvement of conditions in burdened societies for multiple reasons: (*i*) immigrants often support relatives and friends in their countries of origin with remittances; (*ii*) successful immigrants return to, invest in, and become involved in the lives of burdened societies; (*iii*) emigration will tend to put pressure on governments in burdened societies to improve their policies and encourage citizens not to leave or to return if they have already left. In any event, supporting the freedom to migrate is plausibly seen as a matter of justice to individual migrants themselves.[34]

John Finnis has suggested that the intrinsic and instrumental value of cultural cohesion and shared identity provides a reason for states to limit the freedom to immigrate, and that they might reasonably be understood to be able to engage in this kind of limitation in light of a right to control their territory similar to a private owner's right to control her property.[35] It is not clear that individual deliberators in a cosmopolitan original position would embrace borders at all or that, if they did so, they would regard the use of those borders to enforce immigration restrictions as acceptable. Finnis's position will be plausible, in any case, only if we regard states or peoples as reasonably treating "their" territory as "their" property, something that, given the substantial disanalogies between private owners and states, seems difficult to defend.

Richard Miller argues that "[i]f immigration restrictions keep outsiders from joining the civic enterprise through policies that would worsen the lives of members, they are [instances of] justified defense against intrusion, like a nomadic band's refusal to take in outsiders whose joining would be burdensome."[36] But it must still be determined whether those in control of the political apparatus in a given community are entitled to use force to prevent those members of the community who *do* wish to welcome immigrants from doing so, using their own property and resources; whether those who would benefit from migrants' arrival should be denied the opportunity to do so; whether the migrants' own interests are automatically trumped by those of current members; and whether any and all features of current members' lives are entitled to forcible protection.

### F. A Law of Persons Might Incorporate a More Robust Guarantee of Liberty Than the One That Figures among Rawlsian Norms of Domestic Justice

Individual deliberators—at the global or the subglobal level—would have good reason to include a more capacious general guarantee of freedom among the basic liberties than Rawls maintains they would, at least in his later work.

In the final version of his theory of domestic justice, Rawls incorporates a quite limited guarantee of liberty—essentially, a "general presumption against imposing legal and other restrictions on conduct without a sufficient reason."[37] He expresses the "hope that the liberties that are not counted as basic are satisfactorily allowed for by the general presumption against legal restrictions, once we hold that the burden of proof against those restrictions is to be decided by the other requirements of the two principles of justice."[38] But while a freedom counted among the lexically prior *basic* liberties can only be restricted to protect another basic liberty, there is no such limit on the restriction of the nonbasic liberties; it seems, then, that the guarantee of liberty Rawls ultimately defends is, as a general matter, rather weak.

In Rawls's earliest work, he defended a maximizing account of the basic liberties. Everyone, he maintained, has "an equal right to the most extensive liberty compatible with a like liberty for all."[39] He had already opted for slightly different language by the time he wrote *A Theory of Justice*, maintaining that everyone "is to have an equal right to the most extensive *total system* of equal basic liberties compatible with a similar *system* of liberty for all."[40] But, in response to what he acknowledged as an incisive critique offered by H. L. A. Hart,[41] he opted for what he regarded as a more restrictive, but more defensible, account.

As Hart noted, Rawls's earlier formulations bore an evident resemblance, surely not unintentional, to the one famously offered by Herbert Spencer in *Social Statics* as the Law of Equal Freedom: "every man may claim the fullest liberty to exercise his faculties compatible with the possession of like liberty by every other man."[42] Hart sees this sort of language as vague and indeterminate and as incapable of sustaining some plausible judgments. And it is hard not to share his doubts. But perhaps, nonetheless, we can achieve greater determinateness and greater extensiveness without falling into the difficulties Hart underlines.

Rawls's understanding of the basic liberties in *A Theory of Justice* is that these liberties serve to safeguard people's diverse, unenumerated *interests*, and not merely their exercise of the two moral powers.[43] And this may suggest, at any rate, the value of a more open-ended account of the basic liberties. Even if Rawls was right in his later work to question the ways in which he had formulated the first principle of justice in *Theory* and the articles preceding it, pegging the basic liberties to the two moral powers wouldn't be the only way of dealing with the problems Hart noted. Noting that a liberty should be treated as basic if parties in the original position would opt to safeguard it in order to make possible people's pursuit of their various projects would be another.

A fairly straightforward way of doing this would be to preclude nonremedial interference with the architectonic basic liberties—protections for bodily integrity and property (both personal and productive). The ability to benefit from most or all other liberties depends on one's bodily integrity. One couldn't consistently prize other liberties while endorsing an attenuated conception of bodily integrity, because one couldn't enjoy those other liberties while one's bodily integrity was nonconsensually violated. Property rules play a similar architectonic role. They create space within which personal discretion can be exercised, and they specify boundaries that make it easier for conflicts to be peacefully resolved.

Deliberators in the original position might have reason not only to endorse these liberties but also to preclude interference with them except to prevent, end, or remedy interference with others' similar liberties. Liberty generally would be assured, then, in virtue of the robust limits on constraints on these safeguards, which offer substantial space for the exercise of autonomy. In effect, the protections of bodily integrity and property would enjoy lexical priority in relation to the other basic liberties. The basic liberties would be equal in that no scheme of such liberties would be reasonable that did not treat everyone as entitled to the same liberties. But the liberties themselves would not be treated as equal in relation to one another, since the architectonic liberties, needed to ensure the pursuit of people's particular interests, could not be traded off against the other liberties.

Of course, treating these liberties as basic would simultaneously provide robust safeguards for the other fundamental liberties—notably freedom of thought, religion, association, and expression. The proposed account of limitations on the architectonic liberties would, for instance, rule out the imposition of penalties *ex post* predicated on the contents of religious or other expression, since such expression with disfavored contents would not as such constitute or cause harm to others' bodily integrity or property. Similarly, liberties guaranteed in accordance with this account would safeguard freedom of religion and association, since property rights would offer people secure spaces within which religious and other associations could function. And safeguarding the other basic liberties by means of the architectonic rights would provide clear and simple mechanisms for resolving conflicts over religious expression, association, and other basic liberties.

This sort of approach would thus feature general, universal, public rules that would create extensive space for the pursuit of people's various projects. It would not, however, be subject to the same sorts of objections noted by Hart, because it would allow for restraints on and remedies for trespasses and other torts involving harms to bodies and property.

The Difference Principle need not be swallowed up by a maximizing conception of the basic liberties: it could constrain, among other things, choices among potential property rules made in light of information regarding these rules offered by sociology, economics, and related disciplines. While these rules, once adopted, would be robust and not subject to ongoing interference in the interest of particular distributional outcomes, what the rules might be in the first place could perfectly well be shaped in light of the Difference Principle. Obviously, deliberators in the original position would know neither their own preferences nor the contingent distribution of preferences throughout the population. But they would be able to take broad trends into account, noting, for instance, the contribution certain rules could be expected to make to the general availability of primary goods and the distributional consequences of general rules. A scheme of basic liberties elaborated in view of the need to safeguard people's opportunities to realize their diverse interests would ensure significant space for liberty. It need not be framed in maximizing terms, nor need it leave open the sorts of counterintuitive consequences to which Hart understandably objects. But it would certainly open up significantly more space for the pursuit of people's goals than the formulation Rawls offers in his later work while featuring an intelligible principle of limitation.

### G. A Law of Persons Would Protect a Broader Range of Human Rights Than a Law of Peoples

Rawls's Law of Peoples includes multiple human rights protections, but it doesn't safeguard rights Rawls regards as narrowly liberal. It is easy to see multiple reasons for this choice. His people-based starting point, in tandem with his desire to include decent nonliberal peoples in a Society of Peoples, explains why liberal rights are excluded. And, while his starting point is problematic, for reasons I have been at pains to highlight, it's clear why he is, and ought to be, concerned to limit the use of sanctions and military interventions and to foster a consensus at the global level at least in support of *some* human rights.

Cosmopolitan liberals obviously have no reason to dismiss these concerns, especially since sanctions and military interventions are, precisely, violations of multiple human rights to, for example, bodily integrity and freedom of trade (presuming, as I argue later in Part II, that this should be seen as important). And cosmopolitans will have no reason to reject Rawls's concerns with global consensus from a pragmatic standpoint. But they may likely be more inclined than Rawls to regard the fundamental *point* of reflection on global human rights as the formulation and articulation of the rights people *really have*, whether or not the recognition of those rights seems imminent. They will thus opt for a cosmopolitan starting point for reflection on global justice—one that views persons as morally and politically equal despite their territorial affiliations.

A Law of Persons generated through the use of such a starting point can be expected to include, at minimum, the rights Rawls agrees would be acknowledged at the domestic level, since cosmopolitan deliberators would reason in the same way as Rawlsian domestic deliberators. But the list of human rights acknowledged at the global level might well be more expansive than Rawls's official domestic list—though not more expansive than a Rawlsian domestic list presumably *should* be. There would be good reason for it to include basic economic liberties, freedom of global migration and trade, and a general guarantee of liberty—liberty safeguarded by treating what I have called the architectonic liberties as particularly robust. A Law of Persons would not be a license for roving interventionism on the part of high-minded (or not-so-high-minded) states, but it would clearly articulate global norms liberals could embrace without hesitation or qualification.

### III. A Law of Persons Would Feature Robust Limits on the Use of Force

#### A. *Combatants and Noncombatants Would Enjoy Significant Protections under a Law of Persons*

A Law of Persons might be expected to impose more extensive limitations on the use of force than a Rawlsian Law of Peoples. A people-based Rawlsian Law would contain substantial limits (Section B). But a cosmopolitan Law of Persons would likely treat protecting particular persons as more important than protecting the territorial integrity of peoples or maintaining the power of existing regimes (Section C). In particular, it would likely prohibit or radically limit the use of nuclear weapons (Section D). And, given its relative lack of concern with peoples as opposed to persons, it would be less likely than a Law of Peoples to allow a "supreme emergency" exception to just war norms (Section E).[44] In the course of violent conflict, individuals could be expected to fare better under a Law of Persons than a Law of Peoples (Section F).

#### B. *Rawlsian Just War Norms Are Extensive*

Rawls's own version of the Law of Peoples embodies much of traditional just war doctrine.[45] It precludes wars of aggression and requires that a just peace be acknowledged as a central goal of any war and that well-ordered societies wage war where possible in ways that "foreshadow . . . the kind of peace they aim for and the kind of relations they seek."[46] Those who plan aggressive wars are criminals, but civilians and low-ranking soldiers are not and should not be treated as responsible for their leaders' decisions. The human rights of opponents should be respected, and efficiency considerations may ordinarily be used to justify military action only if all the other norms for warfare have been observed.[47]

Thus, Rawls's Law of Peoples would condemn the use of nuclear weapons against Japan as well as the firebombing of Tokyo during World War II.[48] Similarly, the Allied bombing of Dresden resulted from a "failure of judgment" caused by "the passion and intensity of the conflict."[49] However, a Rawlsian Law of Peoples would contain a "supreme emergency"[50] exception that permits direct attacks on noncombatants under limited circumstances.[51] And Rawls would allow the use of nuclear weapons to restrain predatory outlaw states.[52]

### C. Cosmopolitan Just War Norms Would Focus on the Protection of Particular Persons

A Law of Persons, framed by individual deliberators, would be designed to be fair to individual persons. There is reason to think that it might be more likely to provide them with more protection than a Rawlsian Law of Peoples.

Individual deliberators might well not want, given that they would be more likely than not to turn out to be noncombatants outside the veil of ignorance, to be targeted as sacrifices for the putatively greater goods of "civilized life" and "constitutional democracy."[53] They might well be particularly unenthusiastic about being maimed or killed in the course of a state's efforts to protect its own, or another state's, territorial integrity, when doing so wasn't necessary to defend any actual person's body or possessions.[54] And individual deliberators could be expected to be unwilling to endorse rules that treated them equivalently whether they were or were not responsible for causing or threatening harm.

Individual deliberators might not, of course, reason in this way. A deliberator might judge, for instance, that the use of force to topple a violent, authoritarian regime would have a good chance of benefiting her were she a subject of the regime, and that, if the regime could only be removed through the use of violence targeting noncombatants under limited circumstances, she would be willing to tolerate a rule permitting such violence given the limited odds that she would be among the targeted noncombatants.

A great deal would turn, of course, on how individual deliberators assessed the likelihood of the relevant sorts of risks—in very general terms, of course—and on how risk-tolerant, in turn, they proved to be. While they would doubtless wish to minimize the risk of violence to themselves as much as possible, they might opt to do so in multiple ways. If they did choose to endorse the full range of traditional just war norms—norms more demanding than those Rawls envisions as incorporated in his version of the Law of Peoples—it would have to be because they anticipated generically specifiable circumstances persistently warranting these norms on a broad range of risk estimates and tolerances or because they judged it important to encourage people to be noncombatants where possible.

Rawlsian deliberators would, by hypothesis, seek to minimize the damage done by large-scale violence to their societies, while tolerating some putatively necessary harms to individuals along the way for the benefit of those societies, viewed as collectives. Given that the rules embraced by Rawlsian deliberators are already stringent, and that individual deliberators could be expected to be more concerned, in general, with their own well-being as particular persons, they could thus be assumed to favor significantly more stringent constraints on the use of force. On the assumption that the Law of Peoples should contain the robust constraints endorsed by individual deliberators, adhering to these constraints would be a matter of justice and so, in turn, of maintaining a society's political-moral integrity,[55] as also the integrity of individual actors within the society.[56]

### D. A Law of Persons Would Likely Feature More Limits on the Use of Nuclear Weapons Than a Law of Peoples

A Law of Persons could thus be expected impose more severe limits on, among other things, the use of nuclear weapons than a Rawlsian Law. As devices of terror, *strategic* nuclear weapons are characteristically designed for attacks on civilian population centers, which would clearly be precluded by the principle of noncombatant immunity. Because of the indiscriminate character of such weapons, they would almost certainly cause excessive and unjustifiable harm to noncombatants even if used against military targets. While the principle of noncombatant immunity does not preclude foreseen but unintended harm to noncombatants, it would surely rule out the use of high-yield weapons against military targets, which are characteristically limited in size, given the risks to noncombatants associated with strategic nuclear attacks on military targets and given that weapons posing little or no threat to surrounding civilian populations could deliver all the firepower necessary to disable any ordinary military target. A Law of Persons would likely rule out the ordinary use of *tactical* nuclear weapons as well, even against military targets, because of, among other things, the effects of fallout on noncombatants in the vicinity of military targets and a variety of long-term environmental effects.[57]

Thus, in particular, a Law of Persons could be expected to impose stringent constraints on the rights of well-ordered societies to use or threaten to use nuclear arms to restrain outlaw states and to prevent such states from employing weapons of mass destruction against others.[58]

A Law of Persons might, in principle, legitimate deception of outlaw states, so the fact that the use of nuclear weapons was inconsistent with such a Law would not imply that societies with such weapons were prohibited from threatening their use without intending actually to use them. However, if an outlaw state knew that a society adhered to the Law of Persons and knew that this Law prohibited the use of nuclear weapons, it would understand that any threat by that society to use nuclear weapons would be a bluff it could afford to ignore. The bluff would therefore likely be ineffectual.

In addition, if nuclear weapons are maintained at all, there is always the risk that they will be misused—or stolen, and potentially detonated, by terrorists or outlaw states. Given this risk, together with the fact that a Law of Persons might well preclude most or all uses of nuclear weapons, there would be good reason to retain few if any such weapons.

### E. A Law of Persons Would Be Less Likely to Feature a "Supreme Emergency" Exception Than a Law of Peoples

A Law of Persons might be more inhospitable to Rawls's "supreme emergency" exception to traditional just war norms than would Rawls's own preferred Law. This putative exception, as one critic summarizes it, "gives any nation a right to use any means whatsoever to save itself."[59] Rawls does not spell out in detail when a supreme emergency might be said to occur, and he makes clear that disregarding the principle of noncombatant immunity "cannot be justified by a doubtful marginal gain."[60] But he maintains that intentional, deliberate attacks on German civilian populations during the early years of World War II, for instance, were justified for two reasons: "First, Nazism portended incalculable moral and political evil for civilized life everywhere. Second, the nature and history of constitutional democracy and its place in European history were at stake."[61]

The implication, though Rawls does not spell it out clearly, is that *targeting* German civilians was essential to the defeat of Nazism and the preservation of civilization and constitutional democracy.[62] It is surely at least an open question whether this was so. But even supposing it was, we may still ask whether this warranted what has generally been taken to be the evil of direct attacks on civilians.

On what I take to be a defensible moral theory, it did not.[63] But even a Law of Persons, as my description of it has already suggested, might not contain Rawls's supreme emergency doctrine. It would not, at any rate, likely contain a version of this doctrine permitting attacks on noncombatants *simply* to preserve the independence of a people or the survival of a regime. Suppose this doctrine is understood as allowing the use of unlimited force to preserve a state as a political entity or ensure its continued control over its territory. If so, it is hard to believe that individuals uncertain of their places in given societies or their fates would accept it. Doing so would mean allowing the unlimited use of force against the noncombatants in other societies *whom they might also turn out to be* outside the veil of ignorance. If this is so, then adopting a cosmopolitan starting point would be enough to rule out this exception as unjust. But it may be worth attending to the limited arguments Rawls actually offers for his position to highlight their untenability.

Rawls rejects the more rigorous traditional just war requirement that (as he has it) "the innocent" or (as I should prefer) noncombatants (with the understanding that politicians directing combat operations count as combatants) may never be directly targeted. He dismisses the traditional just war view, familiar from Augustine and Aquinas, as a guide to the actions of the liberal political leader.[64] He alleges, without argument or citation, that the principle of double effect—traditionally invoked to warrant the distinction between justified and unjustified killing in war—derives from a divine command rather than from reason.[65] He identifies the Walzerian supreme emergency exception to just war rules as part of the array of politically liberal views he defends but offers very little defense for this view,[66] relying instead primarily on assertion.[67] We do not know simply because Rawls has told us so that the supreme emergency exception *is* just. He does not provide a great deal of argument for the conclusion that it is.

He seems to have in mind the view that the political leader in a liberal society should regard the preservation of her society and her regime as trumping other considerations. It does not seem obvious that this should be so in light even of a Rawlsian Law of Peoples. Her *society* might persist (even if not in its current form) despite the collapse of her regime, and it is hard to see the latter on its own as justifiably treated as supremely important. So the supreme emergency exception would be available, if at all, only when not just a government or regime but *an actual society* faced annihilation. Even here, it is not obvious that Rawlsian deliberators would be inclined to accept noncombatant targeting, or other violence engaged in pursuant to a Rawlsian supreme emergency exception, if the violence putatively licensed by the exception seemed likely itself to destroy one or more societies. This would seem to place a limit on the reach of the exception even in Rawls's own terms.

Perhaps Rawlsian deliberators would regard the principle that the survival of every society must be ensured as nonnegotiable. But it is not certain that they would do so, given that Rawlsian deliberators at the domestic level do not embrace a similar constraint on the use of force.

In any case, Rawls says the political leader in a liberal society "must, *in extreme cases*, be able to distinguish between the interests of the well-ordered regime he or she serves and the dictates of the religious, philosophical, or moral doctrine that he or she personally lives by."[68] The stateswoman is apparently required to give pride of place in her loyalties to the well-ordered society she serves (different, again, from the political regime within which she is an actor).[69] The very survival of that society and of the way of life it embodies are important enough that the society, if threatened by an unjust aggressor, may violate persons in ways that would otherwise be unreasonable.

But the political leader who declines directly to attack noncombatants need not choose to treat the claims *of some comprehensive doctrine* as trumping those of her society. Instead, she is better understood as refusing to allow the claims of her society to trump those of the noncombatants she refuses intentionally to attack. She is not treating her society as less important than an abstract ideal; she is instead refusing to give it absolute allegiance, to treat it as if its interests justified her disregard for the rights of all persons. Her actions might be inconsistent with her political duties; but, even if this were so, it wouldn't follow that they were inconsistent with her Rawlsian natural duties.

The judgment that attacking noncombatants in a "supreme emergency" is appropriate may follow inescapably from the contracting procedure Rawls has outlined. If so, however, I think this provides us with a reason to question this procedure itself in the course of achieving Rawlsian reflective equilibrium. I think, indeed, that one might claim just as readily that the seriousness with which a society regards its fundamental normative commitments is evident precisely when it refuses to disregard them in its own interests.[70]

## F. A Law of Persons Would Likely Provide More Protection for Particular Persons during Violent Conflict Than a Rawlsian Law of Peoples

War is by far the most dangerous and destructive thing states do.[71] And states are all too likely to engage in violent conflict for multiple reasons. For instance, states' political leaders reap enormous rewards for military successes, they can externalize the costs of going to war on taxpayers and conscripts, and they can use military contracting to enrich grateful cronies. These sorts of incentives are structural—essentially inescapable as long as there are states at all. So treating states, or peoples, as foundational at the global level leaves in place institutions that are inherently very dangerous to actual persons. A cosmopolitan Law of Persons would be framed by deliberators quite capable of taking the dangers of war to real individuals into account and as treating those individuals as more important than peoples' claims to control territory or regimes' desires to remain in office. Thus, it would likely offer noncombatants more protection than a Law of Peoples. It would be less likely to contain a supreme emergency exception than would a Rawlsian Law of Peoples. It would likely prohibit the actual or threatened use of nuclear weapons under almost all circumstances. A Law of Persons is defensible on its own terms. But the fact that it tracks traditional just war norms better than Rawls's alternative may be seen as an additional reason to prefer it to his view in wide reflective equilibrium.

## IV. Human Rights Set the Terms for Liberal Responses to Human Rights Violations

### A. *The Rights Incorporated in a Law of Persons Constrain Liberals' Responses to Human Rights Violations*

Liberal human rights protections simultaneously explain why violations of liberal rights are, in an important sense, intolerable *and* why various means of addressing rights violations should be avoided. Nonliberals, including putatively decent ones, may violate multiple rights incorporated in a Law of Persons (as, of course, may putative liberals; Section B). Other rights incorporated in such a Law, together with a range of related moral considerations, preclude governmental military interventions and sanctions in response to nonliberals' rights violations (Section C). Rawls's own approach to grounding toleration is less appealing (Section D). While ruling out sanctions and state military intervention, acknowledging liberal rights doesn't require, and may indeed preclude, more generalized toleration of nonliberal practices, and they leave open various options for responding to such practices

(Section E). Liberals can and should take seriously the limits on force entailed by human rights protections, but they shouldn't give up their commitment to universally shared rights (Section F).

### B. Violations of the Rights Likely to Be Contained in a Law of Persons Are Persistent

A Law of Persons would, as I have argued, feature extensive and robust human rights protections. The rights such a Law could be expected to comprise are all too likely to be violated in multiple settings.

Outlaw states and benevolent absolutisms violate a range of these rights, often by suppressing dissent or using force to impose the tenets of their preferred comprehensive doctrines; burdened societies may do so as well. Decent nonliberal societies protect some human rights, but not others. Their members do not necessarily enjoy full social or legal equality. While diverse religions are tolerated, members of some religious communities may enjoy more privileges than others. Freedoms of expression and assembly may be limited. And sexual minorities may be subjected to various legal disabilities—some potentially very serious.

Institutions in broadly liberal societies might well violate norms contained in a Law of Persons as well. That same-sex sexual conduct was a predicate for criminal liability in various jurisdictions in the United States not much more than a decade ago is a reminder that putatively liberal institutions can disregard human rights in serious ways. And institutions in liberal societies might readily be conceived of as violating other rights (constraining freedom of expression or trade or migration, say), particularly (though not only) if a maximizing conception of the scope of the basic liberties—against which the behavior of these institutions would be measured—is adopted.

Thus, embracing a cosmopolitan Law of Persons means recognizing the potential for a variety of conflicts and challenges related to human rights violations. However, a cosmopolitan Law could be expected to contain resources that would provide some guidance for liberals seeking to respond to such violations.

## C. There Are Good Reasons to Avoid Sanctions and Governmental Military Intervention in Response to Human Rights Violations

Cosmopolitan deliberators would have good reason not to favor the use of sanctions or of governmental military force in response to human rights violations by nonliberals or liberals. Cosmopolitan deliberators will obviously oppose wars, and wartime measures, directly inconsistent with the requirements of justice. But they will obviously also have reason, on prophylactic grounds, to rule out war-related choices that pose significant risks to those they represent.

The use of military force, even when putatively undertaken to protect human rights, is often problematic. It frequently and predictably involves the violation of just war constraints on harm to both noncombatants and combatants—constraints I have already suggested cosmopolitan deliberators could be expected to endorse. And war making often involves conscription, a practice to which individual deliberators will obviously have reason strongly to object because it will usually, whether or not always, violate persons' bodily integrity and rights to author their own lives. (This will be true whether, with Rawls, they regard conscription as itself justified once a war itself is warranted or whether they regard conscription as a species of enslavement and therefore as in principle wrong.)

There are also systemic reasons to favor general prohibitions on states' engagement in military conflicts not involving the defense of their own territories. Such conflicts are predictably associated with human rights violations even when such violations are not integral to prosecuting them, and they pose serious risks to the important interests of many persons. Thus, for instance, they breed resentment that can lead to further violence. They are profoundly, uncontrollably, wastefully expensive, redirecting resources from projects people value and reducing their opportunities to make their own decisions about consumption and supporting or engaging in production. Wars also lead frequently to the implementation of repressive measures, including censorship, propaganda, torture, surveillance, and due process violations of various kinds—which are all too likely to persist after war's official end.

In addition, treating nondefensive military action by states as acceptable creates opportunities for multiple abuses. Putative concern with human rights often masks much less savory objectives actually embraced by politicians—national or personal glory, imperial dominance, or the feathering of the nests of elite cronies; high-flown rhetoric often masks imperial ambition, and would-be empire builders are happy to take advantage of opportunities provided by idealists in order to pursue their own dubious goals.

State decision makers aren't required to cover the costs of warfare themselves; it will thus be especially tempting for them to spend inefficiently: they won't face the same pressures to economize they would if they needed to internalize the costs of their decisions, and they will confront incentives to use the vast sums of money that states at war typically claim to enrich their cronies. Thus, not only will ordinary people be despoiled to fund politicians' war efforts, but resources will be misdirected from the uses to which ordinary people would prefer to put them.

Tax funding for warfare also means that it will be more likely to be carried on a large scale—with more troops, more weapons, more ambitious goals, and more willingness to remain engaged for longer periods. One practical effect is that the scale of destruction will be increased. Another is that mistakes will be more likely, particularly ones involving grandiosity with regard to the potential achievements of military action; state actors can delude themselves into thinking that they can remake a region of the world.

In addition, war making by states helps birth all-too-intimate relationships between politicians, military leaders, and economic elites happily dependent on the money provided to pay for military equipment and other resources. The vast cost of state-driven wars leads to a massive misdirection of resources from productive to unproductive uses, minimizing opportunities for investment in productive activities that provide people with things they actually want and need. And feeding military contractors means creating interest groups disposed to encourage either war or else preparations for war that not only waste resources but also make later wars more likely, since politicians and generals may find it all too tempting to use military assets once they possess them.

Nondefensive state-made wars often violate human rights, and even undertaken to protect human rights, they pose extreme risks to human rights and crucial human interests on multiple fronts. Cosmopolitan deliberators would have good reason to favor general prohibitions on such wars—to rule out specific rights violations characteristically involved in war and to minimize the risks of violations characteristically associated with war. Even defensive wars by states often involve serious injustices; but rules permitting such wars, as long as there are states, would at least be useful in significantly limiting rights violations and minimizing risks of serious harm.

There is good reason to object not only to state-made wars in putative defense of human rights but also to economic sanctions. Sanctions themselves should be seen as constituting abuses of human rights. Sanctions interfere with the freedom of persons to cross, and to provide goods and services across, borders—a freedom cosmopolitan deliberators would have good reason to endorse. They interfere with people's rights to possess, use, and exchange personal productive property. And imposing sanctions characteristically harms the well-being of many people who are not themselves engaged in unjust acts. Sanctions seem consistently likely to harm individuals—often the most vulnerable individuals, and rarely those responsible for the policies to which sanctions are purportedly intended to respond—by denying them the opportunity to obtain very important goods in exchange with others.

A robust human rights regime endorsed by cosmopolitan deliberators could be expected to place significant limits on the means used to address human rights violations. It would rule out the use of both state military interventions and economic sanctions for this purpose.

## D. *Rawls Grounds Liberal Tolerance Unconvincingly in the Equality of Peoples, Concern for the Self-Respect of Decent Nonliberals, and an Analogy with Freedom of Association*

While cosmopolitan liberals would have reason to ground toleration precisely in concern for liberal human rights, Rawls's people-based approach offers a different, and less appealing, set of warrants for toleration.

Rawls does not consider the possibility that liberals might violate human rights. But he does argue directly that liberals should tolerate decent nonliberal peoples. Indeed, the importance of toleration serves as a partial justification for a Rawlsian Law of Peoples as opposed to a Law of Persons.[72]

Rawls does not maintain that liberal and nonliberal institutions and practices are morally on a par.[73] He believes that "a liberal constitutional democracy is, in fact, superior to other forms of society."[74] He does not maintain "that a decent hierarchical society is as reasonable and just as a liberal society."[75] Such a society "does not treat its own members reasonably or justly as free and equal citizens."[76]

However, Rawlsian deliberators would wish to preserve their peoples' equality and would therefore not sanction rules that would permit coercive intervention into their affairs by other peoples.[77] Further, to use sanctions or military force—or even economic incentives[78]—to influence their policy choices would be to violate the self-respect of decent nonliberal peoples.[79] I have already suggested, in the course of arguing against a people-based starting point for global justice, why I find this sort of argument unpersuasive.

Rawls also offers an argument for the generalized toleration of decent nonliberal societies that depends on an analogy with domestic freedom of association: liberals may object on moral grounds to nonliberal patterns of voluntary association but recognize that it is not appropriate to interfere with these patterns by force. Similarly, Rawls suggests, peoples should be free to organize themselves along nonliberal lines, at least if they respect basic human rights.[80]

The analogy is unpersuasive. Liberals may well grant the appropriateness of allowing private discrimination on the basis of gender (as, for instance, in the selection of Catholic priests), even while regarding such discrimination as morally odious. Those engaging discriminatory private conduct must, however, respect just constraints on the use of force. The societies within which they function guarantee a range of rights to their members that provide the backgrounds for their choices to participate in—or abandon—private associations with potentially discriminatory rules of organization or membership. These societies, even if not the associations themselves, are grounded in commitments to equality and freedom, and they can create social arrangements that make the costs of exiting oppressive associations relatively low.

In the same way, liberals belonging to a Rawlsian people whose foreign policy is guided by a Law of Persons can grant that nonliberals may seek human flourishing in diverse ways that liberals reasonably find inappropriate. Liberals need not, however, suppose that norms of justice do not apply to nonliberals or that these norms do not set limits on what they may and may not do. As long as systems of justice are territorially monopolistic and the world's peoples impose barriers on migration, the cost of leaving a particular people will be much higher than the cost of exiting a private association (if, indeed, it is possible to leave at all and if there is somewhere for an emigrant to go).[81] Thus, peoples will not regard unjust arrangements within individual societies with the same sort of tolerance with which they might react to, say, a church's immoral refusal to accept women as ministers.

Even allowing for Rawls's distinctions between peoples and states, peoples are not voluntary associations, and it is not reasonable to model them as if they were. They exercise a degree of power over their members' lives that makes analogies with voluntary associations in liberal societies problematic. Liberals can tolerate such associations precisely because force is not used to preclude exit or sanction the recalcitrant (if it were, they would not, of course, be voluntary).[82] Liberals must obviously take a different view of nonliberal institutions and patterns of life, even decent ones. They must recognize that subjects of a nonliberal people are deprived of what, by their lights, are significant rights, and they will have good reason, within appropriate limits, to seek to help them acquire opportunities to exercise these rights.

If it turned out to be easy not only to leave such a people but also to join another people with a more congenial political, legal, and social order in which one can enjoy a comparable quality of life, a liberal might have more reason than she otherwise would to be sanguine about decent nonliberal peoples' failures to enforce (some) human rights norms. But she would not therefore have reason to regard the failure of nonliberal peoples to protect human rights with equanimity or to abandon efforts to influence such peoples to protect the full panoply of liberal rights.

Persons whose human rights are violated in decent nonliberal societies may suffer significant losses if they immigrate to liberal societies. Leaving a society whose members have a rich sense of communal identity is likely to be costly: it may involve—in addition to significant logistical difficulties—the abandonment not only of a valued community but also of valued relationships with particular persons. The price of living in a society that respects human rights should not be living without important identity-conferring communal and interpersonal relationships.[83]

Suppose liberals were prepared to regard the costs of emigration as acceptable and therefore to view decent nonliberal peoples as comparable to nonliberal associations within liberal societies, at least where those persons whose rights are violated by such peoples are concerned. Even so, not all persons whose rights were violated by nonliberal peoples would be free to emigrate. Many persons with limited resources would not be able to relocate even if they wished to do so—even if no immigration restrictions prevented them from joining new peoples. For them, immigration would not be an option. Thus, the possibility of emigration should not give cosmopolitan deliberators reason to endorse rules that authorized liberals to ignore denials of human rights even by putatively decent nonliberal peoples.

Further, while liberals rightly tolerate nonliberal voluntary associations, they need not regard the exclusionary and subordinative policies and practices of these associations as morally appropriate. Liberals remain free to use various sorts of pressures short of force to affect the behavior of nonliberal associations within their own societies. They would remain free to do the same thing in the global arena. Even if the costs of exiting decent nonliberal societies were minimal, so that those who wished to leave were free to do so, liberals might still, similarly, employ nonforcible means to persuade such peoples to protect the complete array of liberal human rights.

### E. Respecting and Safeguarding Human Rights Would Be Consistent with Various Sorts of Responses to Rights Violations

*1. A Law of Persons Would Permit Liberals to Deal with Human Rights Violations in Various Ways Not Involving Sanctions or State-Made Wars*

Cosmopolitan deliberators would embrace norms that would rule out the use of sanctions or state-made wars as means of securing protection for human rights, while leaving various other options on the table. They would treat some sorts of propagandization as legitimate (Subsection 2). They might endorse some uses of subsidies to promote respect for liberal rights (Subsection 3). And they would have reason to endorse the use of force by nonstate actors in response to violations of human rights (Subsection 4). They would thus treat a wide range of possible responses by liberals to human rights violations as acceptable (Subsection 5).

## 2. Some Uses of Propaganda to Encourage Liberalization Would Be Reasonable

Rawls is surely right that were the liberal members of a global association of liberal and decent nonliberal peoples to use, or seek to use, the resources *of the association* to offer economic incentives to decent nonliberal societies to become more liberal, conflict within the association might well result.[84] Decent nonliberal societies will not want to subsidize propaganda efforts on behalf of ideologies they do not share.

But a Law of Persons would allow, and quite possibly encourage, propaganda efforts by liberals designed to affect the culture and institutions of decent nonliberal societies. Liberals would obviously be open to peaceful challenges regarding their practices, and cosmopolitan deliberators would regard it as a requirement of fairness that such challenges be treated as permissible across the board. Those who violate liberal rights need not be banished from the global system or treated as pariahs.[85] But liberals can still challenge and critique them.

## 3. It Might Be Appropriate to Use Subsidies to Promote Respect for Human Rights

Assuming they embraced taxes and tax-funded subsidies as appropriate, individual deliberators might disagree with Rawls that liberal peoples should not offer nonliberal societies "incentives" to liberalize.[86] Rawls offers two reasons for claiming that such incentives are inappropriate—neither persuasive.[87]

Rawls suggests that the foreign aid programs of liberal peoples should give priority to helping peoples burdened by unfavorable conditions to achieve an appropriate level of economic development.[88] This is not an unreasonable proposal, presuming that such programs should be implemented;[89] but unless this were the *only* focus of liberal societies' aid programs, they could also provide support for liberalization efforts in nonliberal societies, whether or not burdened. Further, social equality and the transparency and accountability of public institutions are likely to promote the economic growth of burdened societies.[90]

Rawls also urges that, because self-determination is valuable, liberal peoples should avoid appearing to coerce nonliberal societies (other than outlaw states and—perhaps—benevolent absolutisms). But offering subsidies is not coercive. Nor is it manipulative. Since, *ex hypothesi*, a decent nonliberal society is not burdened by unfavorable conditions, and so enjoys relative economic well-being, a donor society will not be taking advantage of great economic vulnerability on the part of the recipient people if it conditions aid to a decent nonliberal society on some political or legal reform. It would be perverse, in any case, to maintain that encouraging a society, whether burdened or not, to establish institutions premised on the assumption that people are free and equal violates the right to self-determination of the society for which it was responsible: such institutions are designed to enhance self-determination.

"Decent societies," Rawls says in defense of his position, "should have the opportunity to decide their future[s] for themselves."[91] But offering subsidies is not tantamount to forcible interference. And talk about self-determination here tends, in any case, to ignore the conflict between societal and individual self-determination. After all, what is it for *a society* to decide its future for itself? A society is not one thing, an organism with a unified consciousness and unambiguously shared interests. Rawls's reference to societies as if they were such organisms is a reminder that a Rawlsian Law of Peoples will find it difficult to take the concerns of minority groups and dissenting individuals into account, since it views each people as a unified whole. Rawls's model sometimes seems unrealistically to treat a people as a unitary entity marked by commonality of purpose when in fact there will almost certainly be serious disagreement among the members of a given people regarding norms, rules, and institutions.[92]

To talk about a society deciding its own future is really just to say that some people in the society will make large-scale, vitally important decisions for everyone else. Cosmopolitan deliberators might well view this kind of society-wide decision making skeptically. They certainly would not regard Rawlsian consultation hierarchies as ensuring appropriate respect for the interests of individual members of decent nonliberal societies. (Of course, they might have similar concerns about many or all democratic institutions.) And they would not regard a putative interest in societal self-determination—effectively, the interest of dominant players in retaining their dominance—as warranting the denial of freedom and equal legal rights to its individual members or to restrict their expressive and associational freedoms.

And the problem is further accentuated when, as in Rawls's imaginary decent nonliberal societies, opportunities to affect decision making are significantly constrained, and the interests or views of some sectors of society exert disproportionate weight. The problem is rendered even more severe in virtue of the fact that decent nonliberal (and many other) societies restrict the personal autonomy of (at least some of) their members in ways that prevent them from identifying and exploring their own paths to personal self-determination within the constraints set by others' rights.

*4. The Use of Force by Nonstate Actors to Prevent, End, or Remedy Human Rights Violations Might Sometimes Be Appropriate*

Cosmopolitan deliberators might approve of the use of force to prevent or end violations of human rights in nonliberal (and liberal) societies by *individuals*, à la the Abraham Lincoln Battalion, acting without state funding and authority. Because of the significant differences between their circumstances and those of state actors, their use of force would not be attended by the same risks as state actors',[93] in virtue (for instance) of its scale and funding sources and nonstate actors' inability to externalize costs and avoid liability for their own human rights violations. Thus, presuming they respected appropriate limits on the use of force, it could be perfectly reasonable of them to rescue victims of antigay persecution, ensure immigrants safe passage across state borders, and otherwise resist unjust violence.

Thus, while I strongly oppose state military intervention for reasons I have already noted, I am entirely unconvinced by Jon

Mandle's argument for toleration grounded in a general duty "not to interfere (by using force) with the institutions of legitimate law, including its creation and application."[94] The existence of injustices of the sort with which I have been concerned here will frequently call legitimacy into question. And I am, in any case, doubtful that the concept of legitimacy has any application outside a context in which the imposition of a putative legal requirement on someone is grounded in her *actual* consent either to the requirement itself or to the procedure on the basis of which the requirement is adopted and implemented (except where the requirement tracks an enforceable preexisting moral duty).

At minimum, cosmopolitan liberals should want to say that no putative legal enactment enjoys legitimacy if it significantly infringes on a right that individual deliberators in a global original position would endorse. There will be very good reasons for states not to engage in military intervention in response to such violations, but far less weighty reasons will count against decisions by individuals to do so.[95]

### 5. Liberals Might Reasonably Employ Various Means to Promote and Protect Human Rights

Liberals will not regard tolerance for cultural differences as a sufficient reason to disregard the rights of people violated by nonliberal policies.[96] Cosmopolitan deliberators would accept active advocacy and economic incentivization—whether or not by the *governments* of peoples—as appropriate methods of fostering human rights.[97] And they would also have good reason to see the use of force by nonstate actors as a potentially acceptable means of doing so, because it need not be accompanied by the same risks as state violence. They would embrace a wide range of strategies for human rights promotion— within the limits set by direct and indirect respect for human rights.

### F. Toleration Is Reasonable to the Extent That It Expresses Respect for Human Rights

Taking human rights seriously means regarding violations of these rights as unacceptable whether those violating them are liberals or not. Cosmopolitan deliberators would surely be dubious about regarding nonliberal institutions and policies as worth endorsing or supporting. Liberals should regard such institutions and policies as problematic, perhaps deeply so, and will therefore have reason to challenge and critique them to the extent that doing so seems likely to lead to positive change. Cultural self-respect and the independence of particular societies' political institutions don't provide good reasons for ignoring human rights violations. But it's inconsistent to promote or protect human rights in a way that violates, or promotes the violation of, human rights. Thus, sanctions and state-made wars are unacceptable means of human rights promotion. However, a range of other strategies, including propaganda and the provision of subsidies, might all be appropriate. And liberals might reasonably conclude that liberal individuals and nonstate associations could sometimes justifiably use force to protect persecuted and marginalized people against oppressive governments.

## V. Cosmopolitan Human Rights Norms Would Be Extensive and Robust, Limiting the Use of Force and Determining the Contours of Liberal Tolerance

A Law of Persons would feature the global application of the core requirements of something like Rawlsian domestic justice. At its heart would be the Rawlsian equal basic liberties, along with various additional guarantees defensible along recognizably Rawlsian lines.

Where a Law of Peoples focuses on the concerns and commitments of peoples—though these are, of course, linked to the well-being of their members—a Law of Persons would be designed to safeguard the well-being of particular individuals. Thus, it would feature a wide range of human rights norms applicable across cultures and societies. The rights protected by a Law of Persons would obviously include most or all those safeguarded by a Law of Peoples, but they would also include those Rawls assumes would be protected in accordance with his theory of domestic justice. And, indeed, there is good reason to believe that Rawls's envisioned domestic list is insufficiently capacious—that even more guarantees should be included among the lexically prior basic liberties.

In particular, a Law of Persons could be expected to include limits on the use of force reflective of the importance of life and bodily integrity, which Rawls explicitly acknowledges in his account of domestic justice. Thus, a Law of Persons would likely feature protections against attacks on noncombatants and the use of weapons of mass destruction more extensive than those afforded by a Law of Peoples.

Deprivations of life, liberty, or property would be appropriately tolerated only if consistent with a Law of Persons. But the form an appropriate response to any such deprivation should take must itself be constrained by the requirements that would be adopted by cosmopolitan deliberators in a global original position. Sanctions and the use of military force by states would be ruled out, though various kinds of nonviolent action by states might be less problematic, and the use of force by nonstate actors might be appropriate in some cases. Thus, like a Law of Peoples, a Law of Persons would seek to foster exchange and restrain violence. But it would do so without relaxing its fundamental liberal commitment to the priority of particular persons.

If there is good reason to prefer a cosmopolitan global original position, there is also good reason to think that a Rawlsian account of global justice should be the same in substance as a Rawlsian account of domestic justice. Rawls's official account of domestic justice is, in broad terms, social-democratic. But it's possible to draw on a Rawlsian framework to support quite different sorts of liberal political arrangements. Rawls himself acknowledges that his approach was compatible with various patterns of institutional design by treating both "property-owning democracy" and "liberal democratic socialism" as suitable regime types. But a broader range of possibilities may be seen as acceptable, provided relatively limited modifications in Rawls's theory of domestic justice are accepted and relevant assumptions about human behavior and the human situation are endorsed. I have already begun to suggest how a Rawlsian account ought to be reshaped through an expansion of the range of the basic liberties in a more market-friendly direction.

Cosmopolitan Rawlsians who acknowledge that a global state might be undesirable must show, if they are to defend the applicability of Rawlsian norms of justice at the global level, that these norms don't require implementation by a global state. There is no reason to take a different view at the local level. The existing global order, for all its considerable flaws, provides good evidence that a Hobbesian Leviathan isn't needed to preserve social order and resolve disputes. Cosmopolitans who acknowledge this might have good reason to decline to put their trust in various local Leviathans. I explore this anarchic possibility in Chapter 5.

# CHAPTER 5

# Market Democracy, Market Anarchy, and Global Justice

### I. Cosmopolitanism Can Ground a Broadly Rawlsian Defense of Global Market Anarchy

A cosmopolitan account of global justice can provide normative grounding for a variety of anarchism. It is possible to frame a model of global justice featuring peoples with constrained sovereignty in light of John Tomasi's suggested Rawlsian defense of "free market fairness" (Part II). But a more radicalized version of Tomasi's proposal—one in accordance with which the demands of justice would be compatible with, and might even require, some variety of anarchy—can be effectively articulated in dialogue with Andrew Kuper's somewhat similar suggestion (Part III). A broadly Rawlsian cosmopolitanism can be worked out in anarchic terms (Part IV).

### II. Tomasi's "Market Democracy" Can Be Given Global Expression

#### A. *Tomasi's Revisioning of Rawlsian Domestic Justice Has Global Implications*

A broadly Rawlsian justification is available for a certain sort of classical liberalism, both domestically and globally.[1] Tomasi's arguments for "free market fairness" and "market democracy" point in a potentially useful direction; if these arguments, or similar ones, are defensible domestically, they will be defensible globally as well, and, if embraced by individual deliberators in a global original position, they would lead to robust safeguards for human rights, including economic ones, along with constraints on the global basic structure framed in light of the needs of the least well off (Section B). Implementing a position like Tomasi's at the global level doesn't require a global state, since requirements of distributive justice can be implemented in bottom-up fashion—by, for instance, ending restraints on the free movement of people, goods, and services (Section C). Eliminating such restraints and eliminating protections for unjust privileges would be among the diverse, complementary ways in which well-ordered peoples could assist burdened societies and benefit the globally least well off (Section D); institutions in burdened societies could contribute to benefiting their least-well-off members in similar ways (Section E). Global market democracy could thus involve reshaping the global basic structure in distinctive and effective ways; the result could be a radically classical liberal global order (Section F).

## B. *Tomasi's Market Democracy Is Motivated and Justified in Recognizably Rawlsian Ways*

As I have already suggested when citing Tomasi's proposals regarding the equal basic liberties, his goal is to show why the concerns underlying the Rawlsian framework can and should be expressed in a way that encourages and safeguards economic as well as personal and political liberties. He maintains both that there is good reason to take seriously the concern for the worst-off built into Rawlsian "high liberalism"[2] and, at the same time, that a classical liberal political order of a certain sort can satisfy the concerns underlying the Rawlsian project.

I am, of course, quite aware that Tomasi's proposals have evoked considerable debate among Rawlsians, and I do not wish to ignore their controversial character. This is not, however, the place to defend Tomasi's project in detail; for that, I refer readers to his own work and to the substantial critical literature focused on his book that has already emerged. I want, as it were, to incorporate his arguments by reference here. My goal is simply to sketch his position and suggest some ways in which it could be extended.

Tomasi's approach features two key proposals. He seeks, as I have indicated, to show that the list of lexically prior basic liberties should be expanded to include, for instance, the freedom to acquire, use, and exchange productive as well as personal property. And he argues that the Difference Principle should be applied, and the basic structure therefore shaped, in light of economic and sociological insight into the capacity of markets to provide exceptional benefits for the working poor when compared with other options.

Tomasi's goal is neither to defend a non-Rawlsian approach to political theory nor to amend Rawls's approach in an ad hoc manner. Instead, he seeks to demonstrate that the considerations he adduces in support of the proposals he offers are ones that ought to appear attractive from within the Rawlsian paradigm.

Thus, he argues, as I have noted, that economic liberties meet the criteria articulated by the later Rawls for a liberty's inclusion among the equal basic liberties and suggests that acknowledging such liberties is crucial if the high liberal goal of respecting and fostering individual self-authorship is to be furthered. He emphasizes that the question of what sorts of institutions work most effectively for the working poor can be answered only through the use of careful economic analysis—and not by political philosophy *per se*. It's not a question about policy makers' or philosophers' *intentions* but about the actual effects of various institutional choices. And on that basis, he believes he can show that market freedom is superior to the realistically conceivable alternatives on a consistent basis. He is comfortable with the broad framework of Rawlsian justice as fairness; but he labels his own strand of Rawlsianism "free market fairness." And recognizing that social democracy is ordinarily thought to be the natural expression of Rawlsian justice, he proposes that the approach he has defended, marked by its hospitality to market freedom, should be labeled "market democracy."

I have already sought to note some reasons why a Law of Persons might include not only Tomasi's expanded version of the list of equal basic liberties but, indeed, a yet more capacious version. I will not attempt here to defend his parallel proposals regarding the interpretation and application of the Difference Principle. In this chapter, I offer a development of a Tomasi-style position. Those who tend to be convinced by Tomasi's arguments should find this development appealing—and perhaps, in some cases, even persuasive. Those who are not clear that Tomasi has defended a plausible variety of Rawlsianism may well be skeptical about my radicalization of his approach;[3] my views will doubtless strike them as even more alien than his. But I hope it will also strike them as valuable —as, if nothing else, a potentially provocative continuation of the stimulating conversation Tomasi has initiated.

## C. Global Distributive Justice Is Conceivable without a Global State

Talk about global distributive justice makes sense—as it must if an approach like Tomasi's, or, indeed, any Rawlsian approach, is to be implemented at the global level.

Cosmopolitan Rawlsianism of a market-democratic variety could set the terms for global cooperation and constrain the shape of local institutions. Presuming arguments like Tomasi's are correct, individual deliberators in a global original position would have good reason to treat all the equal basic liberties as rightly available in all societies across the globe; to embrace robust protections for rights to acquire, use, and exchange both personal and productive property across the planet; and to take seriously the economic and sociological evidence that market institutions yield substantial benefits for the poor.

Rawls maintains that individual deliberators at the level of a particular society would agree that, within the constraints set by the equal basic liberties, the Difference Principle should govern the design of institutions affecting the allocation of wealth in their society—the basic structure.[4] If he's right, it seems as if individual deliberators on a global scale would reach a similar conclusion, as Rawls, indeed, assumes that they would.[5]

It may be somewhat too quick to maintain, as Rawls does, that a society's economic performance is primarily a function of "its members' political and civic virtues" rather than its resource endowments.[6] Culture surely matters.[7] But so do institutions, near and far. So do resources. And so does history.

The notion that a society's level of well-being is largely its own responsibility has especially limited application under present nonideal conditions. Factors outside the control of particular societies may have a great deal to do with their wealth or poverty.[8] The design of global financial institutions and trade rules and the manipulation of some societies' political systems by others may continue to limit the economic well-being of poorer peoples in a variety of ways.[9] And some wealth in better-off societies may have been gained in part through past aggression, including aggression directed at those societies now struggling to prosper. The distribution of wealth in *today's* world is to some degree a product of robbery and warfare. So the global basic structure is rightly a focus of significant concern.

Samuel Freeman has argued that the notion of global distributive justice is uninstantiable in the absence of a global state or something similar.[10] On this view, distributive justice governs the actions of *states* in establishing the basic structure of society—in particular, in creating a range of rules governing property, contract, and so forth. The global legal and political environment isn't a basic structure in the relevant sense, because it isn't independent of the policies and legal regimes of individual states and because there is no global government responsible for its features that can be expected to meet the requirements of justice.

If it makes sense to say that implementing global justice requires the operation of elaborate global institutions, in tandem with, say, global schemes of taxation and redistribution, it is easy to see why it might be difficult to pursue this kind of justice at the global level in the absence of a world state. But it is not obvious that the same is true of global market democracy.

An agent need not be required for global (or domestic) distributive justice. Freeman himself is clear that a fully specified set of rules determining, directly or indirectly, who is entitled to what will count as rules of distributive justice. And, while he doesn't favor this approach, he acknowledges that rules that specify that distribution is determined by voluntary exchange could qualify as rules of distributive justice.

Property and contract rules can, in fact, emerge in bottom-up fashion as a matter of evolving social convention, and they can be enforced in a combination of ways that do not require the involvement of the state at any level. It thus seems perfectly reasonable to envision requirements of distributive justice as implemented without the involvement of a global state, in particular. No global hegemon would be needed to implement norms constraining the global basic structure in line with the Difference Principle.[11]

These norms could constrain the relevant rules and institutions in light of the needs of poor societies. Global economic justice could be implemented primarily through the right property and contract rules—though the elimination of privilege and bureaucratic restraint on economic activity and the eradication of restrictions on the movement of people, goods, and services. *Transactional* rules justifiable with reference to (among other things) their distributive significance could emerge and be sustained absent a global state. Uniform rules of this kind couldn't be imposed from the top down, of course, though multiple pressures might lead diverse standards generated on a bottom-up basis to converge. Perhaps a critic might want to argue that, absent uniformity, it wouldn't make sense to talk about *a* global basic structure. But significant overlap in features from legal system to legal system would seem to be sufficient.

Endorsing a cosmopolitan Rawlsianism of a market-democratic variety would mean embracing many features of globalization. For the same sorts of reasons that would prompt them to embrace open markets at the domestic level, particularly in view of the positive consequences for the global poor, cosmopolitan deliberators would embrace a legal framework allowing the unimpeded flow of people, goods, and services around the planet. But they would not treat corporate-led globalization as acceptable. Cosmopolitan deliberators surely would not, for instance, endorse rules allowing polluters to externalize the costs of their activities on the unwilling.

Like polluters, those engaging in long-distance transportation would be expected to internalize the costs associated with their activities, and relocation wouldn't be *subsidized* in other ways, either. It's unclear, then, just what the mix of localizing and globalizing pressures might be. But people would be free to explore the options that seemed most reasonable to them, and people interested in global exchange would surely engage in it.

It seems perfectly possible for, say, freedom of trade and freedom of immigration, both vital contributors to the welfare of poorer societies, to be effected in distributed fashion. Obviously the maintenance of borders open to the movement of people, goods, and services benefits many people other than the least advantaged around the globe, but a crucial justification for free trade and free immigration can and should be their positive consequences for the least well off.

Existing managed trade schemes, serving the interests of dominant political elites, depend on the operation of the bureaucracies associated with the World Trade Organization or needed to effect the provisions of the North American Free Trade Agreement. By contrast, a genuinely *free* trade scheme of the sort required as part of global market democracy wouldn't need such institutions; it could be implemented provided state actors—in both well-ordered and burdened societies—simply got out of the way of migrants and traders.

Truly free trade in goods, services, and labor may be disadvantageous to politically privileged groups. However, given that, as a general matter (assuming the operation of safeguards against force and fraud), it is beneficial across the board, individual territorial monopolists (in a world populated by such entities) would have reason to adopt free trade policies independent of the willingness of others to do so. They would not need to wait for the implementation of any sort of global trade scheme.

The same is true as regards the maintenance of clear, simple, stable property rights and the elimination of barriers to entrepreneurship. Such measures may be undertaken just to benefit the least well off *within* a given society. But they can also benefit, and can be embraced because they benefit, the least well off around the world.

Rectifying the relevant institutional rules can play a crucial role in making various global systems appropriately responsive to the needs of the global working poor. Institutional changes that safeguard free movement and free exchange can serve to implement the Difference Principle.[12] Global economic justice can be effectively fostered on a bottom-up basis.

### D. *Well-Ordered Peoples in a Market-Democratic Order Could Foster the Well-Being of the Least Well Off in Multiple Ways*

Accepting concern for the worst off as a justificatory requirement for a defensible institutional order, an integral element of the

Rawlsian project, is compatible with defending market freedom. Market democracy at the domestic level involves addressing the needs of the least well off by fostering economic freedom within the constraints created by the equal basic liberties. The same approach could and should be involved in implementing the Difference Principle globally.

If a market-democratic global order exhibited the characteristics of a market-democratic domestic order, then income support measures designed to benefit the working poor around the world might be put in place. Governments committed to market democracy would doubtless be aware of the persistent inefficacy and counterproductive character of aid programs.[13] Still, some might nonetheless offer cash assistance to people in such societies. But there are, obviously, other strategies apart from tax-funded wealth transfers they could use to assist burdened societies.

The primary means of aiding the least well off in a market-democratic world would presumably be the liberation of entrepreneurial initiative and the elimination of privilege. The global implementation of robust protections for property and exchange could be expected to sweep away sclerotic bureaucratic constraints on economic activity and empower and enrich many economically vulnerable people.

A world populated by a variety of peoples with their own governments could still be said to have borders. But the acceptance by these peoples of market democracy in tandem with the requirement that all persons be treated as fundamentally equal would presumably mean that deliberators in a global original position would endorse requirements entailing that borders be open.

As I have already emphasized, well-ordered peoples could foster the global redistribution of wealth by opening their borders to free migration and fostering freedom of trade. They could also contribute to the economic circumstances of people in burdened societies by declining to provide military assistance to the governments of these societies. Military assistance plays a crucial role in fostering domestic repression, since militaries are often used against their governments' own subjects; thus, military assistance can tend to minimize dissent and the rectification of large-scale injustice, and thus to keep existing inequities that increase the likelihood of persistent poverty in place. Military assistance also increases the likelihood of military coups. Military dictatorships often resist domestic reform efforts, steal enormous amounts of ordinary people's wealth, and engage in costly martial conflicts—and thus encourage the perpetuation of poverty. And military assistance feeds military machines in ways that may incentivize them to engage in wars. Wars, obviously, promote poverty by killing productive workers, destroying existing infrastructure, and diverting people and resources into unproductive conflicts.

Well-ordered peoples obviously need to avoid military interventions into burdened societies, too. These sorts of interventions have the same destructive consequences, of course, as wars initiated by burdened society governments. In addition, they devour resources in well-ordered societies that could otherwise be used to foster global economic prosperity through investment. And, despite the appealing rationalizations often used to defend them, they serve predictably to serve political and economic interests in well-ordered societies to the disadvantage of ordinary people in burdened societies.

For similar reasons, well-ordered peoples can foster economic well-being in burdened societies by declining to interfere overtly or covertly in these societies' political systems. While it is possible to imagine instances of interference motivated by commitment to genuinely humanitarian goals, licensing interference will open the door to manipulative activities designed, again, to promote the interests of political and economic elites in well-ordered societies. A bright-line prohibition on interference by the governments of well-ordered societies will maximize the chances that these activities will be avoided.

Well-ordered peoples can also foster economic and social improvement in burdened societies by refusing to endorse or protect theft, violence, and political manipulation on the part of multinational firms operating in these societies. They should not shield these firms from legal liability for such abuses, nor should they pressure burdened societies to offer these firms special privileges exempting them from responsibility for their actions or permitting them to engage in aggression against local people and their property. And they should refuse to give effect to statutes of limitations preventing firms from being held accountable for clearly documentable abuses.

The governments of well-ordered peoples could also assist burdened societies by offering reparations for specific acts of violence or theft for which these governments are responsible. This will not always be possible, but where it is possible it will help in potentially significant ways to address the economic circumstances of burdened societies.

Well-ordered societies could also increase the well-being of economically vulnerable people in burdened societies by resisting the temptation to engage in nondefensive military activities. By closing bases and bringing troops home, they would free up resources their citizens could use to invest in economically productive activities that would have positive global consequences. They would also reduce the likelihood of war and terrorism, both of which have devastating economic consequences.

In none of these cases need the Difference Principle be interpreted as a requirement for the creation of a global mechanism of redistribution. The Principle requires us to take seriously the interests of the global working poor as a class when institutions and rules are being designed; it does not necessitate the implementation of specific redistributive schemes by means of well-ordered societies' tax systems. Implementing redistributive schemes in this way could be expected to retard productivity in a way that would render fewer resources available for global investment. By contrast, eliminating privileges and fostering compensation for specific abuses, for instance, would often disperse wealth more widely while keeping property and exchange rules reliable and without reducing productivity by providing excuses for ill-informed bureaucratic tinkering with the economy.

Obviously, we live in a world that is not populated by market-democratic governments. But liberals would still, it seems to me, have good reason to support free trade and open borders as crucial commitments even if many governments didn't immediately choose to do so. Thus, as I have already argued, a global Law of Peoples reflecting the merits of market democracy might well enshrine both commitments as central requirements of global justice.

The persistence of poverty in a world of plenty is obviously among the most pressing moral and political concerns facing the global community.[14] The Difference Principle and the duty to respond to the needs of burdened societies, both of which could be fulfilled by means of the institutional mechanisms I have briefly sketched here, could respond effectively to this concern.

When the Difference Principle is read as requiring tax-funded redistributive schemes, individual governments in a world of peoples might rightly resent being expected to implement the Principle while others declined to do so, as they would likely be expected to do in a world of multiple, independent states. By contrast, reading the Principle in the way I have suggested here need not be experienced in the same way. For at least many of the policies rightly undertaken in fulfillment of the Principle as read along market-democratic lines would clearly and unambiguously yield *mutual* benefit in a way that redistributive schemes might not. Both burdened societies and well-ordered ones, for instance, are clearly better off as a result of genuinely free trade and open immigration policies, with the result that implementing such policies need not be seen as involving long-term costs to or sacrifices by those implementing them.

### E. Authorities in Burdened Societies Could Also Contribute in Multiple Ways to Implementing the Demands of Justice

While they might not always implement these requirements, the Difference Principle as a requirement of global justice would also have implications for the behavior of the governments of burdened societies, given the appropriateness of market democracy as an account of justice at the domestic and global levels. It is not unreasonable to think of the governments of burdened societies as having significant responsibilities to address the problem of the well-being of their worst-off citizens. The fact that they lack resources does not mean that they cannot adopt carefully crafted policies with potentially dramatic effects.

Such societies would fail to take the interests of their economically vulnerable citizens seriously unless they ensured that their legal and regulatory systems did not inhibit productive economic activity by their citizens. Bureaucratic interference with entrepreneurial activity and fruitless attempts at top-down planning both interfere with the well-being of the poor—both those who might otherwise *be* successful entrepreneurs and those who might benefit as workers, customers, or family members from entrepreneurial activity. Robust, reliable property protections and tort and contract rules, by contrast, free from political manipulation, can foster productivity with the potential to yield widespread benefits in burdened societies.

Legal rules that permit foreigners to invest and work in burdened societies on the same basis as citizens and that preclude tariffs and other barriers to trade will also foster greater productivity in those societies. By contrast, when foreign firms are excluded, *or* when they are able to extract special privileges or avoid liability for theft and violence, productivity is hampered.

Burdened societies can help to address the problem of economic vulnerability by ensuring the protection of civil liberties. Free speech, in particular, can ensure the availability of information needed by firms to prosper while also fostering accountability for politicians and corporations and thus reducing the likelihood that state-secured privilege and state-perpetrated and state-tolerated violence will hamper productivity.

Burdened societies could also address the problem of poverty by providing for the return of stolen and engrossed land and other assets or for the provision of fair compensation when return is not possible. Similarly, when land has been engrossed or abandoned, or unjustly transferred to politicians' cronies, burdened societies' governments can help to reduce poverty by declining to interfere with homesteading. These governments could also help to respond to the problem of economic vulnerability by refusing to use aggressive violence against workers seeking to organize.

### F. Market Democracy Can Be Defended Both Domestically and Globally

Market democracy can and should go global. A cosmopolitan version of a Tomasi-style approach to domestic justice would involve extensive liberal human rights protections and limits on the global basic structure that would protect the free movement of people, goods, and services in light not only of the basic liberties but also of the benefits open borders could confer on the members of the least-well-off global class. Tomasi rightly notes that modifications in Rawls's account of the basic liberties and of the Difference Principle could yield a recognizably Rawlsian but distinctive approach to safeguarding economic and other liberties at the domestic level. But individual deliberators in a global original position could be expected to embrace the best arguments on offer at the domestic level—so, if Tomasi's arguments would be persuasive to deliberators in a Rawlsian domestic original position, they would be embraced in a cosmopolitan global original position, too. Tomasi-style free market fairness could be implemented globally in multiple ways, especially through the elimination of privilege, the rectification of past injustice, and the eradication of restraints on the free movement of people, goods, and services across the planet. The result would be a global order that could be implemented and sustained by local institutions and that could be attractive, in particular, because of its capacity to confer substantial benefits on people, including the least well off, in multiple societies. A cosmopolitan version of market democracy could thus be justified and implemented in ways paralleling the domestic version—with evident benefits, as at the domestic level, for the least well off.

## III. Global Market Anarchy Could Be an Appealing Variety of Global Market Democracy

### A. *A Case for Global Market Anarchy Can Be Framed in Terms like Tomasi's*

Tomasi's approach can be extended so that it can be seen as providing grounds not for the minimal statism Tomasi himself defends but, rather, for a variety of market anarchism. He assumes, in effect, that we should begin from within the intellectual frame provided by liberal constitutional democracy, but his statist assumptions can be altered (Section B). Andrew Kuper's polyarchic approach to global order, which can be seen as an excellent representative of the strategies adopted by cosmopolitans disinclined to endorse a world government, hints at the sort of polycentric global order it might be possible to defend along Tomasian lines (Section C). But while

Kuper continues to assume that at least some global institutions will be rooted in the putative sovereignty of territorial monopolists, it is possible to defend a full-blown anarchic conception of global order from which territorial monopolists are entirely absent (Section D). Global market anarchy can be seen as a particularly attractive variety of Tomasi's market democracy (Section E).

### B. *Tomasi's Statist Starting Point for Thinking about Justice May Reasonably Be Modified*

While Tomasi repeatedly refers to the conception of a well-ordered society he defends as "market democracy," the conception of democracy he employs has less to do with elections and parliaments than one might think, and this perhaps suggests a road not taken. "In morally neutral terms, we might say that a society is democratic to the extent that fundamental political power is held equally by all members of that society."[15] But if democracy is to be understood this broadly, as an affirmation of equality of authority,[16] then it can be a feature of a society from which centralized political decision making is entirely absent.

"Webs of private commitments grow as self-authoring individuals interact voluntarily within the framework of public morality,"[17] Tomasi observes. "But," he says, "it is that public framework that defines the moral character of market democracy."[18] If he means that private interactions should take place within the framework of an objective moral order, then he is surely right. But he does not seem to mean simply this. Rather, when he talks about "the framework of public morality," he appears to mean basic rules for social interaction created by democratic political institutions.

A broadly Rawlsian starting point for the construction of requirements of justice seems to presuppose the existence of the democratic state. And I take Tomasi to follow Rawls here. He seems to treat democratic limited government and democratic laissez-faire as the most obvious classical liberal alternatives to standard Rawlsian social democracy because he takes democracy as his assumed starting point and because he treats democracy as a mechanism for managing the state. When he maintains that society is "a public thing," he seems to have in mind the idea that it is unavoidably structured by political institutions—by democratic deliberation.

But this seems to me to be in need of demonstration. A society is perhaps best seen as a set of overlapping and intersecting cooperative ventures.[19] In an important sense, it's an abstraction, a reification. Talk about societies is obviously useful in some contexts, but not if doing so implies the existence of a unified organization, undertaking, or enterprise.

If we reject this conception of society, then it will be more difficult to see a society as a *public*—if that means a *state-shaped*—thing. And we will have reason to doubt whether political institutions are needed at all and to wonder whether people cannot, in fact, create fully consensual, bottom-up structures for the resolution of disputes and the maintenance of social order.

Two converging scholarly literatures suggest that they can. On the one hand, there has been considerable discussion of the potential viability of self-organizing, bottom-up systems of political and legal order. Anarchist social and political theory is thriving.[20] On the other, there is widespread recognition that global legal and economic and social cultural order is, precisely, anarchic.[21] Even as *anarchy* sometimes seems to be a term of opprobrium at the domestic level, it is increasingly used as a neutral characterization of relationships and patterns of activity on the global stage. Just as no final arbiter is required for a national legal system,[22] so none is required globally, either.[23] The relevant literatures are enormous, and I cannot engage with them here as they deserve. I do hope, however, to offer, if nothing else, some provocative suggestions in light of what others have (as I have) argued in detail elsewhere.

## C. Networks of Nonstate Institutions Can Secure Order at the Global Level and Shape the Global Basic Structure

Andrew Kuper has plausibly suggested, in line with many (even if not all) other cosmopolitans, that we need not embrace either Westphalian states (even of Rawls's thin variety) or a world government as sources of global order. Interlocking networks, which need not be territorial in nature, can link people, resolve disputes, and foster relationships in a variety of ways.[24]

Kuper is still inclined to talk about sovereignty, though his preferred variety of sovereignty is concerned with "*kinds* of human practice and resources" rather than with territories,[25] and he embodies the view that "sovereignty can and should be dispersed horizontally and vertically, to multiple levels and loci of authority."[26] His own model appears to assume the persistence of states and treats the various agencies and networks with which he is concerned as, at least, not necessarily consensual.[27] He emphasizes that organizations should embrace nonstate entities as members,[28] while seeming to accept the persistence of what are essentially state-based organizations. But the viability of a model of order maintenance at the global level that doesn't feature a final arbiter ought to suggest that territorially monopolistic states needn't be seen as essential at the subglobal level, either. An emphasis on subsidiarity, a value Kuper happily endorses,[29] obviously militates against centralized power and need not be linked to territorial authority. He urges us to embrace global polyarchy and defends what he calls "Responsive Democracy," linked with a variety of institutions with diverse functions and jurisdictions.

Kuper's approach calls for a range of global institutions, many of them quite distinct from and independent of states. He has effectively highlighted the value of an order that does not depend on states as key sources of global justice; and such a model, serving to undermine robust conceptions of state sovereignty, seems potentially very useful in liberating people from the problematic effects of state action. He does not explicitly consider the possibility of a model that involves doing without the state entirely. But he has also offered no reason to think that the state is necessary to preserving local or global order. Because of the abuses states perpetrate, the dangers they pose, the costs they require people to bear, and their nonconsensual character, a fully *polycentric* legal order,[30] one that abandons territorial monopolists while permitting full exit rights from nonterritorial legal regimes, seems even more appealing than Kuper-style polyarchy.

## D. Global Market Anarchy Can Be Justified as a Variety of Global Market Democracy

### 1. Tomasi's Position Can Be Modified so That It Supports Global Market Anarchy

While Tomasi argues for two varieties of market democracy, which he labels "democratic limited government" and "democratic *laissez faire*," market *anarchy* can be seen as a defensible and particularly attractive variety of Tomasian market democracy—at the global as well as the local level. Deliberators in the original position should reject authority imposed without actual consent—the kind of authority all actual states exercise (Subsection 2). They should opt not to establish or legitimize states because states are persistently and predictably dangerous (Subsection 3). They can be confident that market anarchy need not lead to the ongoing concentration of wealth in a few hands (Subsection 4). They should acknowledge that global market anarchy has the potential, for the same reasons as other varieties of market democracy, to foster the well-being of the least-well-off class (Subsection 5). They should not be inclined to tip the balance in favor of statism by treating a society as a well-integrated cooperative venture—rather, they should recognize, it makes more sense to view any society, global or local, as a network of overlapping and intersecting cooperative ventures (Subsection 6). And they might acknowledge that natural duties are prior to the existence and operation of the state and so can constrain state action and potentially render it illegitimate (Subsection 7). Thus, they can build on Tomasi's market democracy and extend it in the direction of a global market anarchism (Subsection 8).

### 2. Nonconsensual Authority Should Be Rejected in the Original Position

Among equal persons, there is no natural right to rule. No one can rightly assert that she is entitled to dominate any of the others. And this, in turn, suggests that a society in which people's essential equality was understood to ground a commitment to equality of authority might be one in which not only representative political institutions but also decision making by means of some sort of direct democracy could be justifiable only on the basis of actual consent. Elected representatives in representative democracies and majorities in direct democracies claim to exercise authority over other people's lives; what is the putative source of this power? The fact that one person enjoys the support of others is not self-evidently a reason for her to enjoy any legitimate authority over those whose support she does not enjoy.

Rawls does not, of course, treat actual consent as determinative. Political obligation, on his view, emerges from a duty of fair play. But fair play arguments are not obviously successful,[31] and even when successful, they need not be thought to provide much support for the state's claim to authority in a wide range of areas. The appeal of fair play arguments seems to rest on the intuition that it is unreasonable for me to take willing advantage of the benefits conferred by an institution or practice while declining to make a reasonable contribution (financial or otherwise) to supporting that institution or practice. But it is easy to think of many putative government services of which large numbers of people do not take willing advantage—from aggressive warfare to the provision of subsidies and other privileges to favored corporate cronies to the enforcement of prohibitions on interpersonally harmless conduct to the tender ministrations of the carceral state. And even if only receiving substantial benefit, rather than taking willing advantage, is required for a fair play argument to get off the ground, it seems clear that many people do not receive substantial benefits in virtue of many state activities and that the occurrence of the benefits provided by state activities that do offer people acknowledged value is not dependent on state activity and that the state need not be seen as providing these benefits at desirable levels or at desirable costs. In addition, obedience to particular state dictates often fails to contribute in any obvious way to the sharing of the burdens people must supposedly shoulder in order to deliver the putative benefits of state action.[32]

Fair play arguments provide what seems to be an insufficient basis for political obligation, and the reasons this is so would be evident to Rawlsian deliberators. And, indeed, people who value not being dominated might well prefer, behind a veil of ignorance, that political authority not be exercised over them without their consent. State authority fairly clearly lacks a foundation in actual consent. And if this lack of actual consent renders the state illegitimate, then the enterprise of asking what the state ought to do as regards anything, including wealth distribution, is stopped cold in its tracks.

This conclusion may seem unduly extreme, of course, and perhaps it would not be endorsed behind a veil of ignorance. Suppose, alternatively, that the state's nonconsensual character counts against its legitimacy only on a *prima facie* basis: suppose, that is, that there is a presumption against nonconsensual rule but that this presumption could be overcome in some cases for some reasons. The obvious reasons here are the maintenance of social order and the provision of care for the economically vulnerable. Even so, it would be entirely reasonable to ask whether social order can be maintained and the economically vulnerable nourished in the state's absence. Considerable evidence suggests that people can organize themselves to restrain aggression, resolve disputes, and provide social services to the working poor without the involvement of Leviathan.[33] And given both presumption against nonconsensual rule and the multiple risks associated with establishing a state—given states' obvious potential for plunder and war—the fact that the state does not seem to be necessary as a source of social order or care for the vulnerable suggests that supporting the creation of a state or purposefully working to maintain a state's existence would be unreasonable.

Liberal critics of Rawls's approach to global justice have rightly noted the problems associated with assuming that the institutions of decent but nonliberal societies show appropriate respect for particular, dissenting members of those societies. But the particularity of members of *liberal* societies, too, is ignored when dissenters are treated as suitably represented by political institutions despite their disagreement with the comprehensive doctrines underlying those institutions or the substantive policies implemented by those institutions.

A principle treating the requirement of actual—and so, effectively, unanimous—consent either as necessary or else as a defeasible presumption could be reasonable whether or not it was itself unanimously endorsed. It is not inconsistent to require actual consent as a condition of legitimate political authority while recognizing that the principle dictating the need for such consent need not itself be unanimously endorsed to be valid. Because securing unanimous consent to a representative or direct democratic order is likely to be impossible at any given time, and seems even less achievable across generations, a fully consensual political order would be unlikely to be a direct or representative democracy. It would be much more likely to be stateless—to lack any sort of geographical monopolist claiming to control the determination and protection of legal rights. As an alternative to democratic limited government and democratic laissez-faire, we might call it *market anarchy*. Market anarchy can be understood as a species of market democracy, given Tomasi's broad account of democracy. And the Rawlsian approach to justification Tomasi employs can be used to show that market anarchy meets the demands of social justice. (Rawls's own recognition that peoples should abjure claims to full-blown sovereignty might be seen as a faint anticipation of an order in which they abandoned territorially monopolistic claims entirely.)

*3. States Are Dangerous*
Cosmopolitan deliberators should not treat states as necessary, because states are inherently very dangerous. The war making in which they have persistently engaged and to which their taxing power and their leaders' desire for glory and public acclaim render them exceptionally prone, which obviously victimizes the most vulnerable around the world on a persistent basis, is a particularly good example. But the tendency of the state to constitute and serve the interests of an exploitative ruling class provides a further reason to avoid creating, supporting, or maintaining it.

Tomasi grants the importance of public choice analysis of the behavior of state actors.[34] But he does not incorporate the sorts of full-blown class-theoretic analyses that have flourished in the classical liberal and libertarian traditions.[35] This kind of analysis plausibly suggests that the state as a whole is an engine of predation and has consistently been employed for purposes of class exploitation.

Thus, contrary to what both critics and supporters of the modern liberal state often suppose, it is important to emphasize that the state does redistribute wealth—upward, in a wide variety of ways, from massive theft and land engrossment to intellectual property privileges to subsidies to bailouts to licensing rules to building codes to zoning regulations to sales taxes to limits on access to land and capital, all of which tend to make and keep some people poor while enhancing the economic positions of privileged groups. It is in these ways that the state persistently shifts resources to the wealthy and well connected. Eliminating state-secured privilege and remedying state-perpetrated wrongs can thus address the problem of upward redistribution while allowing (in Jeremy Weiland's apt phrase) the free market to eat the rich.[36] What's needed, in brief, is eliminating, rather than strengthening, the state.

A style of class analysis critical of the state provides a reason to be skeptical about the capacity of constitutional constraints on a centralized state to prevent class exploitation. There is no way to rule out exploitative mischief in principle. But the more widely power is dispersed and the less centralized, monopolistic authority enjoys legitimacy in the public's eyes, the fewer opportunities for exploitation seem likely to present themselves.

I have criticized Rawls for being unduly bound to existing institutional arrangements. And perhaps a critic of my claims here might suggest that my arguments could be criticized on similar grounds—that they are unnecessarily focused on current features of political life. But Rawls clearly allows deliberators in the original position to be aware of general social-scientific information. And my claim here is not that, as a matter of fact, some political structures serve elite interests, but rather that political structures can consistently be expected to become increasingly hierarchical and to benefit the wealthy, the well connected, and those likely to benefit particularly from exerting concentrated influence on decision makers. My focus, that is, is not on contingent features of the political scene but on a predictable characteristic of any state structure—something of which cosmopolitan (and, for that matter, domestic Rawlsian) deliberators would have excellent reason to take account.

### 4. Market Anarchy Need Not Foster Wealth Concentration—and Can Lead, Indeed, to Wealth Dispersion

Cosmopolitan deliberators need not opt to legitimize state authority as a means of preventing persistent and irreversible wealth concentration.

Rawls emphasizes that the Difference Principle, implemented at least in part by state redistributive measures, is important to prevent the increasing concentration of wealth in a few hands.[37] Concentrated wealth can simultaneously allow the possessor to gain more wealth in the market, to prevent those other than the possessor from realizing their goals through the political process, and to use the political process to obtain more wealth. But this concern may be less warranted than he seems to think in the absence of the state. If there is no state apparatus to capture, wealth cannot be used to control public culture and limit legal rights, which would instead be safeguarded by a variety of overlapping, consensual institutions with robust exit rights. Similarly, if there is no state apparatus, politically secured privilege cannot be used to obtain further wealth. And in a market freed from such privilege, maintaining wealth concentration—while less troubling in the first place because of the state's absence—would be increasingly difficult.

### 5. Global Market Anarchy Can Foster the Well-Being of the Least Well Off

Cosmopolitan deliberators should take into account the likelihood that a stateless legal order could fulfill the Difference Principle just as a Tomasi-style market democracy could.

Bottom-up social institutions could create and maintain the institutional arrangements that I have already suggested, when focusing on Tomasi's own preferred version of market democracy, could foster the well-being of the least well off. They could maintain social order, deny people opportunities to acquire and retain privilege, and protect freedom of trade and migration. They could preclude, and would not likely engage in, the abuses by states that create and perpetuate poverty. Thus, they could be expected to foster economic productivity in ways that would enhance the well-being of the working poor.

Given that poverty in a generally wealthy society, or in a world in which trade and migration are unrestrained, is in large part structural, and given that structural poverty is a consequence of state-secured privilege and state-tolerated and state-perpetrated mischief, the elimination of the state and the rectification of past and ongoing injustice would deal effectively with the problem of structural poverty. And redistribution effected through the operation of a privilege-freed market could be expected to eradicate the effects of past privilege.

The institutions of market anarchy would not, of course, *guarantee* that any individual instance of economic insecurity or vulnerability on the part of a working poor person would be remedied (any more than other sorts of market-democratic or social-democratic institutions could do so). But they could clearly be seen to do so in a reliable, predictable manner, especially through the elimination of state-fostered structural poverty.[38] And given that legal guarantees themselves—particularly guarantees of economic security—can *undercut* the achievement of the goals they are putatively intended to ensure, the absence of such guarantees need not mean that market anarchy should not be seen as unable to offer well-being to the economically vulnerable.[39]

## 6. Society Can Be Seen as a Network of Cooperative Ventures, Rather Than a Single Venture

Tomasi evidently accepts the Rawlsian view that a society is a cooperative venture for mutual advantage. I have suggested that we can, indeed, view global society in this way, and so we can surely think in the same fashion about more local societies. But while this way of thinking and talking is not simply wrong, it needs to be nuanced if it is to be treated as correct. There are, in fact, multiple cooperative ventures, because there are multiple—innumerable—relationships, networks, institutions, and so forth in which people participate. There is no one clearly demarcated venture in which everyone joins *if* the relevant sort of venture needs to be one such that the participants can reasonably regard its products as theirs to distribute collectively because they all cooperate to make these products. If we are to say that there is, indeed, a single cooperative venture, we can reasonably do so only if *venture* is understood very broadly, loosely, as a metaphor emphasizing people's interconnectedness.

On the standard Rawlsian view, individual deliberators at the domestic level would treat the goods and services generated in their society as shared products of their efforts and so as theirs to distribute. Thus, Rawls's principles of justice seem to be answers to a question something like this: what principles should a collective decision maker employ in determining how collectively owned resources ought to be distributed? But this question appears to presuppose that it is reasonable for any person or group to take responsibility for the distribution of resources in an entire society. I think the metaphor of "cooperative venture" tends to mislead at just this point. People deliberating behind the veil of ignorance might reasonably be expected to ask precisely whether they should be understood as engaged in a common project in the relevant sense—and, I think, to answer "no."

If the resources in a given society are the state's to distribute, then it is surely right that state actors are obligated to avoid making arbitrary distinctions among members of the society. Similarly, the actors who frame a constitutional order for a democratic state can act fairly or unfairly, and the constitutional rules grounding state redistributive activity could thus be said to be fair or unfair depending on the choices of those who framed it. Further, if such a state were responsible for parceling out the product of social cooperation in light of constitutional rules, the framers of these rules could be said to act fairly or unfairly with respect to the distribution of wealth. And in these sorts of cases, (distributive) justice as fairness might well make sense, whether or not precisely in Rawls's own preferred form. But endorsing these hypothetical claims still leaves open various logically prior questions: whether there ought to *be* a society-wide constitutional order, whether that order ought to ground a territorially monopolistic state, and whether resources generated within a society should be seen as the state's to distribute. For, if they aren't, then state actors can hardly be said to act unjustly if they fail to enact something like Rawlsian distributive justice.

The characterization of a society as a cooperative venture for mutual advantage seems to imply that the society has some sort of collective identity. Instead, a society may be seen as the sum total of a vast number of cooperative interactions, including a variety of interlinked ventures. We can speak of a general pattern in accordance with which social cooperation leads to mutual advantage, but that's quite different from a social contract in which people agree to engage in a shared enterprise and determine how best to divide the proceeds of the enterprise. A society is not an enterprise. Social cooperation—extended cooperation involving multiple networks of strangers—does not depend on the existence of the common participation by these strangers in a single, unified legal system or their subjection to a single territorial monopolist. Cooperation among near or distant strangers—including cooperation on what they would acknowledge on reflection to be fair terms— can occur as long as they are linked by the right sorts of conventions and institutions, which can, in turn, be consensual, fluid, and nonterritorial. The importance of peaceful, voluntary social cooperation does not entail the necessity of establishing a territorially monopolistic legal system.

*7. The Priority of Natural Duties and Institutional Requirements Can Be Recast in a Way That Lends Support to the Case for Market Anarchy*

Cosmopolitan deliberators might have reason to treat natural duties as prior to institutional ones and so to support prepolitical (not presocial) property rights.[40]

Rawls supposes that various kinds of principles would be adopted in the original position.[41] He sees the development of principles governing institutions as logically prior to the formulation of principles of natural duty for individuals. But because institutions are more fluid and contingent than the ongoing fact of individual interactions and relationships, it might seem more appropriate to begin with natural duties. And these duties might, in turn, be seen as constraining the appropriate scope of institutional action and authority.

Rawls maintains that "obligations presuppose principles for social forms," while "some natural duties also presuppose such principles, for example, the duty to support just institutions."[42] He embraces the view "that a person's obligations and duties presuppose a social conception of institutions and therefore that the content of just institutions must be defined before requirements for individuals can be set out."[43]

But human interaction can take place without the existence and operation of top-down, monopolistic institutions—the sort it appears Rawls has in mind. The institutions required to maintain social order may be contingent, fluid, consensual, perhaps grounded in bottom-up, spontaneous order rather than in deliberate design. And they can be understood as constrained by natural duties, since these duties can be framed preinstitutionally, and should thus be understood as logically prior to institutions. On this sort of view, institutions will lack any capacity to impose duties on others that couldn't be imposed by the individuals acting within the institutions and as incapable of violating rights (defined correlatively with natural duties) when they couldn't reasonably be violated by those individuals.[44]

Property rules, in particular, can be rooted in natural duties. As long as, in Rawlsian terms, deliberators in the original position would support a given set of rules, these rules can be affirmed as fair. And if they are framed as constraints on institutions, they can be understood as grounding natural duties. The question of what property rules are fair can thus be reached without determining what sorts of more elaborate institutions there should be—without regard to state action. Such rules can thus be seen as logically prior to the state, because they can, in principle, be understood and justified without reference to state action. They can also be seen as prior in another sense, because stable social conventions can ground property rules and the institutions needed to enforce those rules in a complex society.

Deliberators in the original position would have reason to opt for particular property rules in light of their likely impact on the working poor. They would also have good reason to select rules in light of their capacity to promote or embody such values as autonomy, incentivization, peacemaking, reliability, simplicity, and stewardship.

The choices involved in determining property rules can be assessed without regard to the question of the existence of the state, not least since they would apply whether there were a state or not. And the morality of the acts involved in establishing a state and implementing its directives can therefore be assessed against the background provided by the baseline elements of a morally defensible property system. Such a system might not rule out states in principle, but it would, given states' persistent and cronyish interference with people's property, establish a substantial presumption against the creation and operation of states. Together with the other considerations I have noted, they would contribute to making a strong case against the state.

## 8. A Cosmopolitan Version of Tomasi's Market Democracy Can Be Seen as Grounding Global Market Anarchy

Tomasi assumes that a Rawlsian move beyond Rawls to a more market-friendly approach will be a move within the democratic paradigm. And, obviously, if the alternative to democracy is some sort of authoritarianism, there is good reason to avoid transcending democracy. But Tomasi himself points in another direction when he characterizes democracy in a way that suggests that his principal concern isn't with electoral competition or the other surface features of democracy. Given the highly general character of what he says about democracy, it is possible to see market anarchy as fitting within the market democratic model he elaborates.

There are multiple reasons why someone favorably disposed toward Tomasi's basic approach might opt for market anarchy over more conventionally statist market democratic approaches. State authority is nonconsensual (and this ought to be seen as a problem even if the requirement of consent is defeasible). States are dangerous. They aren't necessary to foster the well-being of the least-well-off class. Even under the rule of the contemporary state, a society isn't really a single cooperative venture for mutual advantage: it comprises innumerable cooperative ventures, so that it makes little sense to talk about a "social product" that is ripe for collective distribution by the members of a given (likely state-governed) society; and recognizing this ought to provide some reason not to privilege the state form. (Wealth is, obviously, a product of social cooperation, not of the activities of isolated individuals. But it is not a product of the work of society in the abstract, but rather of the activities of particular cooperating persons who, absent slavery or other coercive institutions and given reasonable transactional rules, cooperate voluntarily and thus have *already* been compensated for their contributions to the production of wealth in their society. To treat them as entitled to *further* compensation would be to engage in double counting.)[45] Natural duties, and correlative rights, can be seen as logically (and, almost certainly, chronologically) prior to the state; thus, while the state may at present serve to define and protect property rights, it isn't needed to do so, and such rights can be invoked to challenge predatory behavior by the state. And, contrary to what its defenders often suppose, the state isn't needed to prevent wealth concentration—rather, in fact, it often, and predictably, serves to *promote* wealth concentration. Deliberators in a global original position would have good reason to embrace worldwide market anarchism.

### E. Global Market Anarchy Can Be Defended as a Superior Form of Global Market Democracy

If Tomasi's market democracy can be defended as a superior variety of Rawlsian legal and political order at the domestic level, then it can similarly be defended as the sort of order that would be chosen by individual deliberators in a global original position. Market anarchy can be seen as a defensible version of market democracy at the domestic level and can thus be defended at the global level. A plausible cosmopolitan account of global justice need not assume the validity of state authority, even democratic state authority. Such an account would mandate consistent, universally applicable human rights; and if individual deliberators in a global original position opted for (the right sort of) anarchy, and so for rights that precluded the establishment of territorially monopolistic political authorities, they would deny legitimacy to monopolistic states anywhere on the planet. Cosmopolitans like Kuper have defended various sorts of global polyarchy; abandoning territorially monopolistic states as necessary features of the global order might be seen as a plausible next step in the development of cosmopolitanism.

### IV. Market Democratic Rawlsianism Can Be Recast as a Normative Basis for Global Market Anarchy

A generally Rawlsian framework could, with limited and defensible modifications, be understood as offering grounds for treating as just and attractive a legal and political order featuring robust protections for productive as well as personal property and an extensive range of choices related to work—a market order. John Tomasi has proposed and defended a range of modifications of the needed sort. But Tomasi's own approach can be radicalized further and cast as a defense of full-blown market anarchy. *Global* market anarchy—which exhibits some similarities to the sort of global polyarchy defended by many cosmopolitans—would be accepted by deliberators in a cosmopolitan original position on the same grounds that more local variants of market anarchy would be embraced by deliberators in less inclusive variants of the original position.

The embrace of global market anarchy as a live possibility would mean, I suggest, the incorporation of one further provision in the Law of Persons: a limit on nonconsensual authority. Rawlsian considerations cannot show that such authority would never be permissible. But given the potential viability of global market anarchy and the undesirability of nonconsensual authority, a Law of Persons would rule out nonconsensual authority when the other requirements of such a Law could be reasonably expected (not guaranteed) to be met in its absence.

Whether global market anarchy would ultimately prove attractive to cosmopolitan deliberators depends, of course, on whether it can be shown that nonstate institutions can effectively maintain social order, resolve disputes, and foster the well-being of the least advantaged. And of course I have only gestured in the direction of the needed sort of demonstration. I hope I have said enough, however, to make clear why a recognizably Rawlsian account of global justice might be cast in market-democratic rather than social-democratic terms, and why market anarchy could be understood as a defensible variety of market democracy.

# Conclusion

The considerations Rawls offers in support of protections for individual freedom and of moral and political equality at the domestic level remain attractive. They seem applicable to persons across our planet just as they do to persons in particular societies already committed to liberal values. A cosmopolitan second original position thus appears to provide a more appropriate means of identifying suitable principles of global justice than its Rawlsian alternative. Persons should be regarded as equal globally from a political and moral standpoint, and principles of global political morality should be assessed in light of the equality and distinctness of persons.

If they were assessed in this way, the result would be a Law of Persons—a standard of global justice and global law rooted in moral egalitarianism. If Rawlsian arguments for the basic liberties at the domestic level are accurate, then the Law of Persons could be expected to incorporate the equal basic liberties Rawls treats as foundational in his account of domestic justice (elaborated to provide robust protections for noncombatants). It should also include protections for the ownership and disposition of productive property and for global freedom of movement, as well as a more general presumption of liberty. And it should preclude nonconsensual authority except where the demands of justice cannot be achieved without the operation of such authority. It would thus be similar to but importantly different from Rawls's proposed Law of Peoples.

As Rawls himself notes, the Law of Peoples is rooted in "an original position at the second level that is fair to peoples and not to individual persons."[1] The fact that representatives of equal peoples are depicted as determining the content of the Law of Peoples plays a decisive role in shaping Rawls's argument.[2] It leads to a stark contrast between Rawlsian norms of domestic and global justice,[3] and between the Law of Peoples and a cosmopolitan standard of global justice. A cosmopolitan view "is concerned with the well-being of individuals."[4] By contrast, a Law of Peoples is designed to foster the well-being of particular peoples and of the Society of Peoples.[5]

Rawlsian arguments for a people-based account of global political morality and to a global order to which separate peoples are central do not seem finally persuasive. A cosmopolitan account offers more substantial grounds for human rights and justice in war. And such an account is, at any rate, hospitable to a global anarchism defensible as a variety of John Tomasi's market democracy.

Rawls's Law of Peoples provides an attractive framework for the international relations of a reasonably just liberal people. Although it does not embody a satisfactory account of global justice, its adoption by even one major power might significantly improve the state of the world, if only by reducing the likelihood of military interventions around the globe. Nevertheless, it is inadequate. For instance, (*i*) it unduly limits advocacy on behalf of freedom and social equality; (*ii*) it leads to unduly minimal global human rights norms, offering insufficient protection, for instance, for freedom of migration and trade; and (*iii*) it seems to license some unwarranted disregard for particular persons in time of war and to give too much latitude to those who might wish to threaten to use or actually employ nuclear weapons.

It is unfortunate that Rawls's sense of what is possible and appropriate is expressed in a global norm designed to be acceptable to deliberators representing states—or, rather, peoples. It is doubly problematic that he seeks to articulate an account of global justice acceptable to decent nonliberal societies when he grants that there are no such societies. He does not suggest, after all, that the Law of Peoples needs to appear attractive from the standpoint of benevolent absolutisms, outlaw states, or burdened societies. His choice to structure a Law of Peoples acceptable to decent nonliberals seems to be responsible both for the specific content of his proposed global norms—for instance, the limited nature of the human rights protections it affords—and for its underlying assumption that peoples rather than persons should be treated fairly at the global level.

If there were good reason for distinguishable geographic territories to be governed by distinct, monopolistic institutions, individual deliberators would decide on a regime of justice with which their continued existence would be consistent. So it cannot be the need to preserve independent peoples that is primarily responsible for Rawls's assumption of the equality of peoples in the second original position. The fact that individual deliberators would opt for norms that the public policies and cultural standards of decent nonliberal societies would violate seems to play a significant role in accounting for Rawls's preference for the starting point he adopts.

The denial that liberals might not wish to *compel* nonliberal societies to enforce the full panoply of liberal rights need not entail the denial that the members of these societies are *entitled* to those rights. And Rawls himself must believe this, since he affirms that a liberal political order is better in some important sense than a nonliberal one.[6] To say this seems to be to say, among other things, that the claims liberals make about human rights are more nearly reasonable than those made by nonliberals—to say *that people do, in fact, have the rights liberals say they do.* But in what sense is this so?

Rawlsians might want to say that these human rights are the guarantees that would be endorsed in a cosmopolitan global original position. They might regard Rawls's proposed (two-stage) second original position as a means of capturing largely pragmatic intuitions about the most effective way for liberal societies to structure their foreign policies, given that global justice as they understand it cannot be immediately achieved.

There are ways of understanding Rawls's approach to global justice, of course, as a predictable, even if not necessary, development of his reconceived account of the grounds of justice at the domestic level. But, whatever the pragmatic appeal of Rawls's own preferred version of the Law of Peoples, it clashes persistently with the liberal moral convictions that made *A Theory of Justice* attractive to many readers. While I have raised questions here regarding Rawlsian political liberalism, this is not the place to critique the work of the later Rawls in a systematic way. But it seems not unreasonable to suggest that, to the extent that problems with Rawls's account of global justice flow from his revised understanding of the grounds of domestic justice (they surely do not do so in their entirety, since Rawls envisioned a people-based approach in *Theory*), that understanding deserves to be rethought. Further support for doing so might seem to flow from the fact that Rawls's own account of moral duties, at least in the context of war, does not seem as readily defensible with reference to his own political conception of liberalism as with reference to his account of justice understood as an independent conception of morality and politics.

In any event, it seems to me that there is good reason, perhaps especially for those who share many of his moral intuitions, not to embrace the starting point Rawls adopts when framing an account of global political morality or the specific normative recommendations that follow from it. The approach he articulates in *A Theory of Justice* remains more appealing as a model for decision makers at the global level than his own preferred global alternative.

What an alternative, cosmopolitan Rawlsianism might reasonably be thought to amount to is, of course, a different matter. Tomasi has underscored the availability of a recognizably Rawlsian understanding of domestic justice that arguably remedies a number of defects in Rawls's own approach. If Tomasi's arguments are successful, then individual deliberators in a domestic original position might be expected to endorse what he calls "market democracy." But it seems to follow that individual deliberators with access to the same sort of information in a global original position could be expected to do the same. Thus, acceptance of a cosmopolitan starting point for reflection on global justice might lead to the endorsement of a market-democratic global order that would set the terms for any subsidiary institutions.

At minimum, this would mean the addition of several constraints to Rawls's envisioned Law of Peoples. A Law of Persons might reasonably be expected to incorporate protections for the unimpeded movement of people, goods, and services around the planet, with limits imposed only by individual property rights and by the requirement that people take full responsibility for the costs they have demonstrably imposed on the unconsenting. For the sorts of reasons Tomasi has suggested, it should also include robust protections for the ownership of productive as well as personal property. It should significantly narrow (when compared with Rawls's own Law of Peoples) the range of permissible harms to noncombatants in the course of violent conflict. It should severely limit the exercise of nonconsensual authority. And perhaps it should also incorporate a significantly more extensive guarantee of liberty than the one Rawls endorses.

Accepting an expansion of the requirements of global justice, as embodied in a Law of Persons, along with the basic framework of market democracy, leaves open the question whether there should be a plurality of states or no state at all. The no-state option is, at any rate, attractive and defensible, even on Rawlsian grounds; if adopted, a market-anarchist conception of global justice would, of course, rule out not only a global state but local territorially monopolies as well, since they would violate the same rights as would a global state and since the institutions needed to maintain social order could prove effective without local monopolists just as they could without a global monopolist. Market anarchy's preferability to the alternatives on Rawlsian grounds will be depend in significant part, I take it, on how successfully it can be shown to be capable of addressing the problems of social order and the well-being of the working poor.

Anarchism and cosmopolitan Rawlsianism might seem like uneasy allies. Rawlsian cosmopolitans often tend to favor the creation of a world state and to view accepting the absence of such a state as at best a concession to human frailty. But anarchism has obvious affinities with cosmopolitanism. It is fundamentally, of course, a cosmopolitan position, denying that people's rights are derived from the decisions of states and rejecting states' claims to sovereignty. And anarchism views the maintenance of social order at the domestic level in much the way cosmopolitans might be thought to view global order in the course of responding to the sovereignty argument against cosmopolitanism-without-a-global-state. Among the considerations appropriately offered in support of anarchism has traditionally been that social order seems to be maintained on the global level without such a world state. Cosmopolitan Rawlsians who reject the sovereignty argument against cosmopolitanism-without-a-global-state might well consider whether the viability of global order without a global state might not also imply the possibility of meaningful talk about justice at any level in the absence of the sort of territorial monopolist Rawls seems to take for granted. Despite the difficulties associated with it, Rawls's approach is certainly worth exploring, both because of its continuing influence in legal and political theory and because of its fruitfulness and its capacity to capture a number of key moral insights. In particular, there is something fundamentally correct and important about treating individual persons as the building blocks of society, and about an account of fairness as nonarbitrariness, and Rawls's account of domestic justice suggests reasons why this might rightly be the case globally as well as domestically.

This is so, I believe, whether or not one is a Rawlsian. It seems to me, though, that Rawlsians in particular have good reasons to be cosmopolitans. Rawlsian moral and political theory has been tremendously influential on academics and policy makers alike, because Rawls's work has captured central and significant features shared by many liberal understandings of justice. I believe, therefore, that it is important to emphasize that Rawls's defense of a people-based model of global justice is unattractive on what many Rawlsians should find appealing grounds.

That doesn't, of course, make a cosmopolitan alternative like the one I have envisioned here non-Rawlsian. I deliberately build on Rawls's own account of domestic justice, arguing for the incorporation of both its starting point and (a modified but clearly recognizable version of) its substance into an account of global justice. A Law of Persons would be a Rawlsian account of domestic justice writ large. It would also be clearly Rawlsian because its specifically economic provisions would be justified with reference to the Rawlsian concern for the least-well-off class, the working poor.

A Rawlsian approach informed by a unified understanding of justice, particularly if modified along the lines Tomasi suggests, would be appealing in multiple ways. Accepting such an approach would mean embracing the moral and legal equality of persons, and thus enhanced respect for noncombatants in wartime, while fostering a global prosperity with the potential to transform the lives of the least well off. It would mean, in short, committing to the creation of a global society governed by a liberating and morally appealing Law of Persons.

# Notes

## Acknowledgments

1. The relevant publications are Gary Chartier, *Peoples or Persons? Revising Rawls on Global Justice*, 27 B. C. INT'L & COMP. L.R. 1 (2004); Gary Chartier, *Reconciling Rawls and Hayek?*, 17 INDEP. REV. 322 (2013) (The Independent Institute, 100 Swan Way, Oakland, CA 94621-1428; http://independent.org).
2. For my own preferred approach to a number of the matters considered here, *see, e.g.*, GARY CHARTIER, ANARCHY AND LEGAL ORDER: LAW AND POLITICS FOR A STATELESS SOCIETY (2013).

## Introduction

1. Favorable references to markets are frequently read, and doubtless frequently intended, as affirmations of the *status quo*—of the existing distribution of property, of current patterns of economic relationship, and so forth. This book is not the right place to stake out my position on this matter. But I do want to underscore the fact that my positive remarks about markets at various points throughout this book shouldn't be understood as endorsements of the rigged and distorted markets prevalent across our planet today; *see* MARKETS NOT CAPITALISM: INDIVIDUALIST ANARCHISM AGAINST BOSSES, INEQUALITY, CORPORATE POWER, AND STRUCTURAL POVERTY (Gary Chartier & Charles W. Johnson eds., 2011).

## Chapter 1

1. *See* JOHN RAWLS, THE LAW OF PEOPLES, WITH THE IDEA OF PUBLIC REASON REVISITED (1999).

2. *See* RAWLS, LAW, *supra* note 1, at 63. *Cf.* JOHN RAWLS, *The Law of Peoples, in* COLLECTED PAPERS 556 (Samuel Freeman ed., 1999).
3. *See* RAWLS, LAW, *supra* note 1, at 23 n.17, quoting JOHN STUART MILL, CONSIDERATIONS ON REPRESENTATIVE GOVERNMENT (J. M. Robinson ed., 1977).
4. Thus, for instance, Native American tribes might qualify as peoples in Rawls's sense; *cf.* Bethany R. Berger, *Liberalism and Republicanism in Federal Indian Law*, 38 CONN. L. REV. 813 (2006); Kristen A. Carpenter, *The Interests of "Peoples" in the Cooperative Management of Sacred Sites*, 42 TULSA L. REV. 37 (2006); Kristen A. Carpenter, *Real Property and Peoplehood*, 27 STAN. ENVTL. L.J. 313 (2008).
5. A group plausibly seen as a "people" might not occupy geographically distinct territories or control their borders; *see* Morgan Cloud, *The Foundations of Law: Human Rights for the Real World*, 54 EMORY L.J. 151 (2005).
6. *See* RAWLS, LAW, *supra* note 1, at 27–28.
7. *See id.* at 29.
8. *See id.* at 17.
9. *See id.* at 27.
10. *See id.* at 35.
11. *See id.* at 29.
12. *See id.* at 27.
13. Thanks to Seana Shiffrin for helping me to see the need to address this issue.
14. *See, e.g.*, JOHN RAWLS, POLITICAL LIBERALISM 27 (1996).
15. Thanks to Kevin Vallier for an exchange on this point.
16. *See* JOHN RAWLS, JUSTICE AS FAIRNESS: A RESTATEMENT 41–42 (Erin Kelly ed., 2000).
17. *Id.* at 42.
18. *Id.*
19. *See, e.g., id.* at 61–72; JOHN RAWLS, A THEORY OF JUSTICE 65–73 (rev. ed., 1999). On the derivation and nature of the basic liberties and the basic norms of justice, see RAWLS, LIBERALISM, *supra* note 14, at 289–371; RAWLS, RESTATEMENT, *supra* note 16, at 39–134; RAWLS, THEORY, *supra*, at 47–101.
20. In the remainder of this book, I'll generally call representatives of *peoples* in the second original position *Rawlsian deliberators*;

I'll refer to a Law of Peoples of the sort to which Rawlsian deliberators would assent as a *Rawlsian Law of Peoples*. I'll label representatives of individual *persons* in an alternative second original position *individual deliberators* and a set of requirements of global justice that contracting individual deliberators might be expected to endorse a *Law of Persons*. I will call a person who supports, or might under at least some circumstances support, a Law of Persons a *cosmopolitan liberal*.

21. *See* RAWLS, LAW, *supra* note 1, at 17, 23–25; RAWLS, THEORY, *supra* note 19, at 331–32. For an alternative interpretation of the cited passages in *A Theory of Justice*, see THOMAS W. POGGE, REALIZING RAWLS 242–44 (1989); Thomas W. Pogge, *An Egalitarian Law of Peoples*, 23 PHIL. PUB. AFF. 195, 205–6 (1994).
22. Since both versions of the global original position Rawls envisions are ones in which peoples rather than persons are represented and since both endorse the same conclusions, this simplification in the text should not, I believe, necessitate any misunderstanding of the heart of Rawls's approach. Rawls employs a simpler, one-stage approach to the formulation of norms of global justice in his initial derivation of the Law of Peoples; *see* THEORY at 331.
23. RAWLS, LAW, *supra* note 1, at 10; *cf. id.* at 82; Charles Beitz, *Rawls's Law of Peoples*, 110 ETHICS 669, 675 (2000).
24. *See* RAWLS, LAW, *supra* note 1, at 11–23. *Cf.* GILLIAN BROCK, GLOBAL JUSTICE: A COSMOPOLITAN ACCOUNT 31 (2009).
25. *See, e.g.*, RAWLS, LAW, *supra* note 1, at 4–5, 58, 85, 89–91, 106.
26. *See id.* at 41. When he first envisioned extending his theory to the global arena, Rawls made much the same point. *See* RAWLS, THEORY, *supra* note 19, at 332–33. However, the norms envisioned in *The Law of Peoples* are more elaborate than those canvassed in *A Theory of Justice*.
27. *See* RAWLS, THEORY, *supra* note 19, at 39–50. Rawls acknowledges that, as their reflection and dialogue are described in *A Theory of Justice*, individual deliberators at the domestic level don't necessarily reflect on all conceivable options and that, were they to do so, they probably wouldn't ultimately endorse the ones he defends; *see id.* at 509.
28. *See id.* at 37–38. Rawls supposes that the fourth principle doesn't apply in all cases. I argue subsequently for a stricter account

of the duty of nonintervention than the one he embraces; *see* Chapter 4.IV.C, *infra*.
29. RAWLS, LAW, *supra* note 1, at 38 (footnote omitted).
30. *See id.* at 64–68.
31. *See id.* at 63–68.
32. *See id.* at 72–73, citing G.W.F. HEGEL, PHILOSOPHY OF RIGHT §308 (1821).
33. *See* RAWLS, LAW, *supra* note 1, at 71–72.
34. *See id.*
35. *See id.* at 72, 78.
36. *See id.* For criticisms of the notion that liberal and decent societies can oblige their members, *see, e.g.*, CAROLE PATEMAN, THE PROBLEM OF POLITICAL OBLIGATION: A CRITIQUE OF LIBERAL THEORY 117–20, 125–29 (2d ed. 1985); MICHAEL HUEMER, THE PROBLEM OF POLITICAL AUTHORITY: AN EXAMINATION OF THE RIGHT TO COERCE AND THE DUTY TO OBEY (2013).
37. *See* RAWLS, LAW, *supra* note 1, at 77 (footnote omitted).
38. *See* RAWLS, LAW, *supra* note 1, at 72 n.12.
39. *See id.* at 75–78; *cf.* Antonio F. Perez, *The International Recognition of Judgments: The Debate between Private and Public Law Solutions*, 19 BERKELEY J. INT'L L. 44, 46 n.13 (2001).
40. *See id.* at 75–77.
41. *See id.* at 75–76.
42. *See id.* at 69.
43. *See id.* at 68–70.
44. *See id.* at 59–60, 74–75.
45. William J. Aceves, *Critical Jurisprudence and International Legal Scholarship: A Study of Equitable Distribution*, 39 COLUM. J. TRANSNAT'L L. 299, 393 (2001) (footnotes omitted).
46. RAWLS, LAW, *supra* note 1, at 17 n.9. *See* Allen Buchanan, *Rawls's Law of Peoples: Rules for a Vanished Westphalian World*, 110 ETHICS 697, 698 (2000); *but cf.* Joel P. Trachtman, *The Law and Economics of Global Justice*, 96 AM. J. INT'L L. 984, 990 (2002).
47. *Cf.* Simon Caney, *Cosmopolitan Justice and Equal Opportunities*, *in* GLOBAL JUSTICE 123, 139–40 (Thomas W. Pogge ed., 2001).
48. *Cf.* A. John Simmons, *Disobedience and Its Objects*, 90 B.U.L. REV. 1805, 1823–31 (2010).

49. Richard Steinberg helped me to see the need to make this point; I am grateful to Seana Shiffrin for forcing me to think about it further.
50. Joel P. Trachtman, *Welcome to Cosmopolis, World of Boundless Opportunity*, 39 CORNELL INT'L L.J. 477, 477 (2006).

## Chapter 2

1. *Cf.* THOMAS W. POGGE, REALIZING RAWLS 247–48 (1989).
2. JOHN RAWLS, A THEORY OF JUSTICE 17 (rev. ed., 1999); *see id.* at 441–49. *Cf.* JOHN RAWLS, POLITICAL LIBERALISM 19, 79–81 (1996); JOHN RAWLS, JUSTICE AS FAIRNESS: A RESTATEMENT 20, 87 (Erin Kelly ed., 2000).
3. RAWLS, THEORY, *supra* note 2, at 442.
4. *See, e.g., id.* at 18–19, 42–45, 104, 507–8; RAWLS, LIBERALISM, *supra* note 2, at 28.
5. *See* RAWLS, THEORY, *supra* note 2, at 507.
6. One way to think about this might be to ask whether the assumption of a closed society is simply an analytical convenience or whether it is integral to Rawls's account of domestic justice. Rawls obviously assumes the inescapability of states (or "peoples"), and he obviously thinks of membership in a people as morally significant. But it seems to me that he also acknowledges a more fundamental moral equality that is in some tension with this assumption.
7. JOHN RAWLS, THE LAW OF PEOPLES, WITH THE IDEA OF PUBLIC REASON REVISITED 82–83 (1999).
8. *Id.*
9. *Id.* at 83.
10. *Id.*
11. In a broad sense, of course, this is true of contractarian theories of all sorts (thanks to Carole Pateman for this point); these theories characteristically embody accounts of reasoning, motivation, and circumstance that constrain the kinds of outcomes to which they can be expected to lead. This kind of circularity is not necessarily a fatal flaw in Rawls's argument. However, given his argument's circular character, it provides little *additional* support for his starting point. *See, e.g.*, CAROLE PATEMAN, THE PROBLEM OF POLITICAL OBLIGATION: A CRITIQUE OF LIBERAL THEORY 7, 14–20 (2d ed. 1985).

12. RAWLS, LAW, *supra* note 7, at 60.
13. *Cf. id.*
14. *Id.* at 32. *Cf. id.* at 32 n.35, 69 n.8.
15. *See id.* at 32.
16. *Cf.* SIMON CANEY, JUSTICE BEYOND BORDERS: A GLOBAL POLITICAL THEORY 82 (2005).
17. Of course it need not be seen as begging the question against Rawls's theory of domestic justice to the extent that Rawls has successfully defended political obligation *in that theory*. See, *e.g.*, JOHN RAWLS, *Legal Obligation and the Duty of Fair Play*, in COLLECTED PAPERS 117 (Samuel Freeman ed., 1999). But there is little reason to embrace either consent or fair play arguments or other grounds characteristically proffered for a duty to obey the state; *see* MICHAEL HUEMER, THE PROBLEM OF POLITICAL AUTHORITY: AN EXAMINATION OF THE RIGHT TO COERCE AND THE DUTY TO OBEY (2013).
18. RAWLS, LAW, *supra* note 7, at 34. While Rawls's language evokes his constructivism, since he doesn't elaborate a constructivist argument for anticosmopolitanism here, I treat this potential justification for his people-based starting point in Chapter 3 rather than Chapter 2.
19. *See id.* at 33–34.
20. *Id.*
21. *See id.* at 23–25.
22. *See id.* at 17 n.9, 82.
23. *Id.*
24. *See id.*
25. *Id.* at 83.
26. *Id.* at 61.
27. *Cf.* BRIAN LEITER, WHY TOLERATE RELIGION? (2011).
28. Harry D. Gould, *A Response to Professor Brilmayer on Rawls*, 6 INT'L LEGAL THEORY 42, 44 (2000) (alteration in original). Gould says a cosmopolitan standard would render decent nonliberal societies "morally illegitimate." I've referred to injustice in the text because of the specific sense, different from this one, in which Rawls is inclined to talk of illegitimacy.
29. *Id.* at 44.
30. *See* RAWLS, LAW, *supra* note 7, at 62, 83; *cf.* CHARLES LARMORE, THE MORALS OF MODERNITY 146–51 (1996).

31. *See* Gary Chartier, *Righting Narrative: Robert Chang, Poststructuralism, and the Possibility of Critique*, 7 ASIAN PAC. AM. L.J. 105, 116–17 (2001).
32. Charles Beitz, *Rawls's Law of Peoples*, 110 ETHICS 669 (2000), considers and rejects as circular the argument that "a cosmopolitan approach would necessarily be less tolerant of the diversity of political traditions and cultures." After all, the question at issue is in part precisely "whether or to what extent international institutions and the foreign policies of liberal states should tolerate nonliberal cultures." *Id.* at 681.
33. RAWLS, LAW, *supra* note 7, at 62; *cf.* Gould, *supra* note 28, at 44.
34. *See* RAWLS, LAW, *supra* note 7, at 62.
35. *See id.*
36. *See id.*
37. *See id.* at 61–62; *cf.* Mark Tushnet, The Law of Peoples *by John Rawls*, 38 ALBERTA L. REV. 1069, 1073 (2001) (book review).
38. This is true, similarly, if acting justly *isn't* required for self-respect. If this is so, it doesn't follow that being characterized by others as unjust might not harm their self-respect. Suppose, say, that the people who are not acting justly think they are acting justly and believe that acting justly is necessary for self-respect. Then being characterized as unjust by others might make them lose self-respect. But if self-respect is simply understood as a nonmoralized category, one to which acting justly isn't necessary, it's not clear why we should be overly concerned about it. And it would seem that, in this case, bringing about the loss of self-respect might nonetheless be warranted as a means of fostering just institutions. Thanks to David Gordon for pressing me to make this point.
39. This is almost certainly not Rawls's view, since he is concerned, in general, not with self-respect as an attitude but with *the social bases* of self-respect—which I take it he understands in such a way that it is an appropriate response to the existence of these bases. *Cf.* RAWLS, RESTATEMENT, *supra* note 2, at 59–60. I note this alternative only for the sake of completeness.
40. An anonymous reader observes that the expectation that this disapproval not be announced would be inconsistent with the public character of the justification Rawls seeks for the Law of Peoples. But publicity in the relevant sense is a means of

fostering stability, so this should be seen as a concern of nonideal theory, not as a constraint on what ought to count as a theory of justice in the first place. Nonideal theory might in some cases be concerned rightly with stability and so might rightly dictate that it was imprudent or rude to criticize certain morally objectionable practices in nonliberal societies, even though those practices were clearly condemned by ideal theory. Further, the moral principles on the basis of which disagreement is voiced could be clearly and publicly articulated, even if a regime declined to draw the relevant conclusions in an equally public manner.

41. *Cf.* Tushnet, *supra* note 37, at 1074–75.
42. *See id.* Rawls's belief that liberals ought to respect decent nonliberal societies does not depend on the conviction that decent nonliberal institutions are as satisfactory as liberal ones. *See* RAWLS, LAW, *supra* note 7, at 62.
43. *Cf.* Thomas W. Pogge, *Rawls on International Justice*, 51 PHIL. Q. 246, 248 (2001).
44. *See* RAWLS, LAW, *supra* note 7, at 69–70. Rawls rightly notes that various kinds of decision-making mechanisms may exist in different kinds of organizations, but that we may nonetheless regard these organizations as equal for some purposes. But this observation could be challenged, for instance, on the basis that a university is easy to leave, while a state is not.
45. *See* Tushnet, *supra* note 37, at 1074; Frank J. Garcia, *The Law of Peoples*, 23 HOUS. J. INT'L L. 659, 667 (2001); John M. Finnis, *Reason, Revelation, Universality, and Particularity in Ethics*, 53 AM. J. JURIS. 23, 43 (2008). Charles Beitz suggests that Rawls may be arguing "that a people should be treated as having special ethical significance because its flourishing as a people is essential to its capacity to manage its human, material, and cultural resources, and, thus, to sustain its institutions, for the benefit of present and future members." Beitz, *supra* note 32, at 682. But a cosmopolitan could justify treating peoples as having "special ethical significance" and responsibility for particular spaces or institutions without conceding that the principles of global justice should reflect the conclusions of Rawlsian rather than individual deliberators; *see id.* at 683.
46. *See* RAWLS, LAW, *supra* note 7, at 39.

47. *Cf.* Pogge, *Justice, supra* note 43, at 248.
48. *See* Thomas W. Pogge, *The Incoherence between Rawls's Theories of Justice*, 72 FORDHAM L. REV. 1739 (2004); Lea Brilmayer, *What Use Is John Rawls' Theory of Justice to Public International Law?*, 6 INT'L LEGAL THEORY 36, 38–39 (2000). *But cf.* Gould, *supra* note 28, at 43 (the well-being of individual "people [is] the guiding concern" in *The Law of Peoples*).
49. *Cf.* Pogge, *Justice, supra* note 43, at 247.
50. *See* RAWLS, LAW, *supra* note 7, at 82.
51. *Id.* at 17 n.9.
52. Fernando R. Tesón, *The Rawlsian Theory of International Law*, 9 ETHICS & INT'L AFF. 79, 85 (1995) (italics supplied).
53. *Id.*
54. Richard W. Miller, *The Interests of the Governed and the Interests of Humanity: The Moral Importance of Borders*, 90 B.U.L. REV. 1785, 1787 (2010). *Cf.* Joel P. Trachtman, *The Law and Economics of Global Justice*, 96 AM. J. INT'L L. 984, 989 (2002).

## Chapter 3

1. *See* Véronique Zanetti, *Global Justice: Is Interventionism Desirable?*, *in* GLOBAL JUSTICE 204, 209 (Thomas W. Pogge ed., 2001). Zanetti notes—*see id.* at 208—the idea that global society is not a cooperative venture for mutual advantage as one of the rationales invoked by Rawls for his refusal to endorse a cosmopolitan original position, but she doesn't provide any textual support for the claim that Rawls says this explicitly.
2. *Cf.* Andrew Hurrell, *Global Inequality and International Institutions*, *in* GLOBAL JUSTICE, *supra* note 1, at 32.
3. *See* PATRICK HAYDEN, JOHN RAWLS: TOWARD A JUST WORLD ORDER 98 (2002); Thomas M. Scanlon, *Rawls' Theory of Justice*, 121 U. PA. L. REV. 1020, 1066–67 (1973) (thanks to Howard Chang for this reference).
4. *Cf.* ALLEN BUCHANAN, JUSTICE, LEGITIMACY, AND SELF-DETERMINATION: MORAL FOUNDATIONS FOR INTERNATIONAL LAW 84 (2004) (noting the existence of a global basic structure).
5. JOHN RAWLS, A THEORY OF JUSTICE 7 (rev. ed., 1999).
6. *Cf.* Anthony D'Amato, *International Law and Rawls' Theory of Justice*, 5 DENVER J. INT'L L. 525 (1975).

7. Kok-Chor Tan challenges the view that existing social cooperation needs to meet some minimum standard for Rawlsian requirements of justice to apply globally. Even if the rules of the current global game are rigged, so that global interactions often do not foster mutual advantage, we can see the vision of the entire world as a cooperative venture as a solidaristic aspiration reflective of the essential moral equality of persons; see KOK-CHOR TAN, JUSTICE WITHOUT BORDERS: COSMOPOLITANISM, NATIONALISM, AND PATRIOTISM 56–61 (2004). Tan suggests that people can treat the establishment and maintenance of just institutions as linking them in a cooperative venture even if they are not already participating in such a venture. See id. at 60. Whether this approach is finally adequate is not a question I will seek to resolve here; but if it is, of course, the objection I have considered will be unsustainable.
8. See JOHN RAWLS, JUSTICE AS FAIRNESS: A RESTATEMENT 5–8 (Erin Kelly ed., 2000); RAWLS, THEORY, *supra* note 5, at 4; *cf.* RAWLS, RESTATEMENT, *supra*, at 50, 95–96; JOHN RAWLS, POLITICAL LIBERALISM 15–16, 391 n.27 (1996).
9. See RAWLS, RESTATEMENT, *supra* note 8, at 7.
10. See RAWLS, LIBERALISM, *supra* note 8, at 15.
11. See JOHN RAWLS, THE LAW OF PEOPLES, WITH THE IDEA OF PUBLIC REASON REVISITED 36 (1999).
12. Perhaps some such analysis lies behind some observations offered in (at least partial) explanation of Rawls's preference for peoples over persons; see Lea Brilmayer, *What Use Is John Rawls' Theory of Justice to Public International Law?*, 6 INT'L LEGAL THEORY 36, 38 (2000). But this makes little sense as a basis for an account of *justice*.
13. Zanetti, *supra* note 1, at 210.
14. A variety of ad hoc nongovernmental arrangements might obviously be embraced; see, e.g., Roger E. Rustad Jr., *What Lessig (Almost) Gets*, KURO5HIN, Oct. 5, 2002, http://www.kuro5hin.org/story/2002/10/4/23856/9235 (arguing for an international treaty governing unsolicited bulk commercial email).
15. See Edward Foley, *Human Rights Theory: The Elusive Quest for Global Justice*, 66 FORDHAM L. REV. 249, 263 (1997); *cf.* Joel P. Trachtman, *The Law and Economics of Global Justice*, 96 AM. J. INT'L L. 984, 991 (2002).

16. *See* Allen Buchanan, *Rawls's Law of Peoples: Rules for a Vanished Westphalian World*, 110 ETHICS 697 (2000).
17. Harold Hongju Koh, *Why Do Nations Obey International Law?*, 106 YALE L.J. 2599, 2603 (1997) (footnote omitted).
18. *See generally* THOMAS M. FRANCK, FAIRNESS IN INTERNATIONAL LAW AND INSTITUTIONS (1995).
19. *See* Koh, *supra* note 17, at 2645–58.
20. I argue for this point subsequently.
21. Rawls emphasizes that, at the domestic level, the principles of justice qualify, in general, as collectively rational even when ignored by large numbers of people who must thus be coerced to cooperate. *See* RAWLS, THEORY, *supra* note 5, at 505.
22. *Id.* at 434–35; *cf.* Trachtman, *supra* note 15, at 989. Of course, if certain psychological characteristics of a population make a particular scheme of justice difficult to implement, this might be an especially strong argument against implementing it, despite its attractiveness on other grounds; *see* BERNARD WILLIAMS, ETHICS AND THE LIMITS OF PHILOSOPHY (1985).
23. Whether this is so depends in part, of course, on just what the requirements contained in a Law of Persons—as opposed to those included in a Law of Peoples—might be. For instance, if a Law of Persons required top-down redistribution by some global authority—something not mandated, in general, by the Law of Peoples—a Law of Persons could prove more difficult to implement. However, the Law of Peoples does require *some* redistribution, even if not the kind of redistribution often thought by Rawlsians to be required at the domestic level. And it is not clear that *this* kind of redistribution would, in fact, be required by a Law of Persons; *see* Chapter 3.IV.C and Chapter 5.II.C, *infra*.
24. Joseph Heath, *Immigration, Multiculturalism, and the Social Contract*, 10 CAN. J.L. & JURISPRUDENCE 343, 347 (1997), argues that "even if social contract principles would recommend a system of global relations in which freedom of movement among nations was guaranteed, there is no reason to think that such principles should be respected by any state in the absence of an effective institutional structure that can provide reasonable guarantees of compliance among the others." But of course they *should* be respected (*i*) because their moral appeal doesn't

depend on universal acceptance and (*ii*) because of the general advantages of open borders *to societies with open borders.*
25. RAWLS, LAW, *supra* note 11, at 80–81.
26. *See id.* at 37.
27. *See* RAWLS, THEORY, *supra* note 5, at 98–101, 293–301.
28. RAWLS, THEORY, *supra* note 5 at 333; *cf.* Gregory C. Keating, *Reasonableness and Rationality in Negligence Theory*, 48 STAN. L. REV. 311, 321 n.40 (1996).
29. RAWLS, THEORY, *supra* note 5, at 333. Given that he believes that a soldier might offer a justification rooted in natural duty for refusing to do something the soldier judges to be immoral, Rawls's purpose in referring to treaty obligations seems to be to note a *further* justification that the soldier might offer for conscientious refusal. He does not suggest, I think, that a soldier would be free to, say, violate the principle of noncombatant immunity in a given case if no treaty provision constrained her conduct in that case.
30. *See id.*
31. *See id.* (characterizing justice in war).
32. *Id.* at 98; *cf.* Jeremy Waldron, *Redressing Historic Injustice*, 52 TORONTO L.J. 135, 138 n.11 (2002).
33. RAWLS, THEORY, *supra* note 5, at 99. This idea might seem more at home in the intellectual world of *A Theory of Justice* than in that of *Political Liberalism.* But the political conception of justice as fairness is still, in a limited but important sense, a moral conception. A proponent of political liberalism, as Rawls characterizes and defends this idea in his later work, might be able to accept the notion of natural duties, provided that these duties were understood and justified as part of a political conception.
34. Thanks to David Gordon for underscoring the need to make this point.
35. RAWLS, LAW, *supra* note 11, at 3.
36. *See* RAWLS, LIBERALISM, *supra* note 8, at xviii.
37. *Id.* at 36–68; RAWLS, RESTATEMENT, *supra* note 8, at 3–4, 40, 84.
38. *See* RAWLS, LIBERALISM, *supra* note 8, at xviii–xx.
39. *See id.* at xvii–xxxiii.
40. *Id.* at 143 (footnote omitted).

41. *See id.* at 141–42.
42. *See id.* at 36–68; RAWLS, RESTATEMENT, *supra* note 8, at 3–4, 40, 84.
43. RAWLS, LIBERALISM, *supra* note 8, at 147.
44. *See id.* at 158–68.
45. *See id.* at 166–67.
46. *Id.* at 156.
47. *Id.* at 147–49.
48. *Id.* at 169; *see id.* at 169–71.
49. *See id.* at 148.
50. *Id.* at 143.
51. *Id.* at 386–87.
52. *Id.* at 386.
53. *Id.* (italics supplied).
54. *Id.* at 387 (italics supplied). Rawls's language here might appear to require unanimity in support of a shared conception. But he doesn't seem to require unanimity elsewhere; *see id.* at 65. A full unanimity requirement at the domestic level would seem to push him in an anarchist direction in which he hardly seems likely to want to go.
55. *Id.* at 390 (footnote omitted).
56. *Id.*
57. Rawls suggests that concern with the problem of stability lies at the root of his position's post-*Theory* development. *See generally id.* at xvii–xxxi, xxxix–lxii.
58. *See* Leif Wenar, *Why Rawls Is Not a Cosmopolitan Liberal, in* RAWLS'S LAW OF PEOPLES: A REALISTIC UTOPIA? 95, 102–4 (Rex Martin & David A. Reidy eds., 2006).
59. *Cf.* JOHN RAWLS, *The Law of Peoples, in* COLLECTED PAPERS 529, 549–50 (Samuel Freeman ed., 1999).
60. Leif Wenar, *Contractualism and Global Economic Justice, in* GLOBAL JUSTICE, *supra* note 1, at 76, 84.
61. BUCHANAN, JUSTICE, *supra* note 4, at 42.
62. *See* RAWLS, LIBERALISM, *supra* note 8, at 168, 390.
63. *See id.* at 161.
64. *See id.* at 162.
65. *See id.*
66. *Id.* at 163.

67. CHANDRAN KUKATHAS, THE LIBERAL ARCHIPELAGO: A THEORY OF DIVERSITY AND FREEDOM 66 (2003).
68. *See* RAWLS, LIBERALISM, *supra* note 8, at 163.
69. *See id.* at 165.
70. *See id.* at 165–68.
71. Despite the way Rawls seems sometimes to frame things, it is hard to say that all comprehensive doctrines would be likely to endorse even the bare-bones structure of the original position at the domestic level. He acknowledges that it may be necessary to insist, in practice if not explicitly, that doctrines calling for political violence are incorrect. *See id.* at 152–53.
72. Alternatively, of course, they might simply reject or reformulate these underlying principles because of their undesired implications.
73. *See* RAWLS, LIBERALISM, *supra* note 8, at 225.
74. The idea of public reason is a specifically politically liberal idea. *See* RAWLS, LAW, *supra* note 11, at 143–44. Rawls introduces a more constrained variety of global public reason that isn't liberal; *see id.* at 54–59.
75. Thanks to David Gordon for this point.
76. RAWLS, LAW, *supra* note 11, at 59; *see id.* at 54–58.
77. RAWLS, LIBERALISM, *supra* note 8, at 226.
78. *See* HAYDEN, *supra* note 3, at 92.
79. This turn is elaborated particularly in JOHN RAWLS, *Kantian Constructivism in Moral Theory*, *in* COLLECTED PAPERS, *supra* note 59, at 303; and *idem*, *Justice as Fairness: Political Not Metaphysical*, *in* COLLECTED PAPERS, *supra*, at 388.
80. An anonymous reader's interpretation of Rawls's position has considerably enriched my thinking about Rawlsian constructivism, and I have drawn freely, and gratefully, on it throughout my discussion of this topic here.
81. Rawls's analogy between personal equality at the domestic level and the equality of peoples at the global level—*see* RAWLS, THEORY, *supra* note 5, at 332—may be seen as supporting this reading of his intent. Alternatively, this passage may be seen, not as an *argument* for the design of the second original position, but simply as a brief elaboration of the principles that might form part of a Law of Peoples (though he doesn't use the term) and as

an example of the unsurprising congruence between such a Law and currently accepted norms of international law.
82. Wenar, *supra* note 58, at 107.
83. Wenar, *supra* note 58, at 109. Wenar might prove to be right, though I am skeptical, that we cannot do without states. But he is surely *not* right that we need an account of global justice that permits states to use force to maintain control over their territory, as over against doing so to protect the bodies and possessions of specific people. It will be reasonable to safeguard the latter using force, but not to prevent secession or to assert control over unoccupied territory.
84. *See id.* at 137 (footnote omitted) (italics supplied).
85. RAWLS, RESTATEMENT, *supra* note 8, at 27 (emphasis added).
86. RAWLS, LIBERALISM, *supra* note 8, at 65.
87. *Id.*
88. *Id.* at 65–66.
89. *See id.* at 66.
90. *See* RAWLS, LAW, *supra* note 11, at 105–13. Rawls implies that not all burdened societies afford even the minimal human rights protections intended to be secured by the Law of Peoples; *see id.* at 109–10.
91. *See id.* at 94–97; RAWLS, THEORY, *supra* note 5, at 332–35. John Simmons suggests that these sorts of Rawlsian duties can be cast as duties for liberal citizens; *see* A. John Simmons, *Disobedience and Its Objects*, 90 B.U.L. REV. 1805, 1820–21 (2010).
92. *See* RAWLS, LAW, *supra* note 11, at 91. *Cf. id.* at 81 n.26, 93 n.6.
93. *See id.* at 93 n.6; *cf. id.* at 80–81.
94. *See* Wenar, *supra* note 58, at 106–10.
95. Wenar, *supra* note 58, at 108.
96. *Contra* Wenar, the cosmopolitan who makes this move is not "affirming that national boundaries and state membership are morally arbitrary, while also conceding that these are practically indispensable." *Id.* at 110. The cosmopolitan need not regard states as practically indispensable; she may simply maintain that, given that they are currently in existence, their actions ought to be limited by requirements of justice that apply universally. And were she to concede that they were practically indispensable (as I would not), she need not regard this as fundamentally arbitrary in a way that vitiated her cosmopolitanism, since

cosmopolitan rules of justice could still rightly limit the actions of states.
97. *See* THOMAS NAGEL, *The Problem of Global Justice*, *in* SECULAR PHILOSOPHY AND THE RELIGIOUS TEMPERAMENT: ESSAYS 2002–8 at 61 (2010); Richard W. Miller, *The Interests of the Governed and the Interests of Humanity: The Moral Importance of Borders*, 90 B.U.L. REV. 1785, 1798–99 (2010). My focus is on the sort of argument someone taking a position like Nagel's or Miller's might offer, rather than on the specifics of Nagel's or Miller's own position.
98. *Cf.* Miller, *supra* note 97, at 1800.
99. *See* Chapter 4, *infra*.
100. *See* Philip Pettit, *Rawls's Peoples*, *in* REALISTIC UTOPIA, *supra* note 58, at 38.
101. *Id.* at 48.
102. *Id.*
103. *See id.* at 49–50.
104. *Id.* at 51.
105. *See id.* at 50–51.
106. *Id.* at 52.
107. *Id.* at 51.
108. *Id.*
109. Thanks to David Gordon for emphasizing the potential attractiveness of reading Rawls in this way.
110. *See* Robert Nisbet, *The Pursuit of Equality*, PUBLIC INTEREST, Spring 1974, at 103, reviewing JOHN RAWLS, A THEORY OF JUSTICE (1971).
111. *See, e.g.*, John M. Finnis, *Reason, Revelation, Universality, and Particularity in Ethics*, 53 AM. J. JURIS. 23, 41 (2008); Miller, *supra* note 97, at 1791–92.
112. *See* RAWLS, LAW, *supra* note 11, at 62. *Cf.* Samuel Freeman, *Frontiers of Justice: The Capabilities Approach vs. Contractarianism*, 85 TEX. L. REV. 385 (2006). *But cf.* Fernando R. Tesón, *The Rawlsian Theory of International Law*, 9 ETHICS & INT'L AFF. 79, 98 (1995). Being a relativist about *justification* need not, of course, make one a relativist about *truth*; *see* JEFFREY STOUT, ETHICS AFTER BABEL: THE LANGUAGES OF MORALS AND THEIR DISCONTENTS 24–28, 93–94, 244–55 (2d ed. 2001).
113. RAWLS, RESTATEMENT, *supra* note 8, at 39.

114. *Id.* at 5.
115. *Id.* at 7 (emphasis added).
116. *Id.* at 19. *Cf.* Richard M. Rorty, *Postmodern Bourgeois Liberalism*, 80 J. PHIL. 583 (1983); Richard M. Rorty, *The Priority of Democracy to Philosophy*, *in* PROSPECTS FOR A COMMON MORALITY 254–78 (Gene Outka & John P. Reeder Jr. eds., 1993). Rawls is not incapable of giving aid and comfort to those who want to see his project in a way Rorty (in these essays) would find congenial; *see, e.g.*, JOHN RAWLS, *The Independence of Moral Theory*, *in* COLLECTED PAPERS, *supra* note 59, at 286, 289–91.
117. It obviously would not do to note that, on this interpretation of Rawls, the principles in question would be ultimately arbitrary and unwarranted: the sort of relativism implied in this interpretation suggests that *all* deep normative judgments are similarly relative, including the contention that it is inappropriate for liberals to act with respect to nonliberals on the basis of liberal principles.
118. *Cf.* letter from Oliver Wendell Holmes to John Gray (Sept. 3, 1905), *quoted in* SHELDON NOVICK, HONORABLE JUSTICE: THE LIFE OF OLIVER WENDELL HOLMES 283 (1989), *quoted in* ALBERT W. ALSCHULER, LAW WITHOUT VALUES: THE LIFE, WORK, AND LEGACY OF JUSTICE HOLMES 24 (2000).
119. There are good reasons for them not to do so. *See, e.g.*, Gary Chartier, *Righting Narrative: Robert Chang, Poststructuralism, and the Possibility of Critique*, 7 ASIAN PAC. AM. L.J. 105, 118–21 (2001).
120. RAWLS, LIBERALISM, *supra* note 8, at 62 (emphasis added).
121. RAWLS, LAW, *supra* note 11, at 62.
122. *See id.* at 74–75.
123. This sort of point might be framed with regard to truth or, more cautiously, in terms of reasonableness. It seems clear that the later Rawls would not have wanted to rest any of his argument on claims about truth. It does not follow that a sufficiently robust version of reasonableness couldn't do much the same work.
124. The same argument for equality is articulated in RAWLS, THEORY, *supra* note 5, at 441–49; RAWLS, RESTATEMENT, *supra* note 8, at 19–20.
125. RAWLS, RESTATEMENT, *supra* note 8, at 5 n.5 (emphasis added).

126. *Id.* at 31.
127. Holmes, letter to John Gray, *quoted in* NOVICK, *supra* note 118, at 283, *quoted in* ALSCHULER, *supra* note 118, at 24.
128. *See* RAWLS, LIBERALISM, *supra* note 8, at 44–46.
129. Further, even if the validity of claims for liberal political morality were ultimately grounded in nothing more than a Western consensus, this would have no implications for the particular choices made by liberals. If all norms are culturally dependent, liberal states remain perfectly free to act on the norms prescribed by *their* culture; relativism affords no support for tolerance. If liberalism dictates that its adherents pressure other societies to create liberal institutions and embrace liberal norms, the fact that liberalism is understood as a Western idiosyncrasy gives liberals no reason to ignore their "can't helps" when determining how best to interact with decent nonliberals. If liberal principles demand effort and sacrifice from liberals, recognizing that these principles were fundamentally arbitrary might lead liberals to choose less strenuous alternatives. But this would be a reflection of liberals' preference for sloth, not of the support for tolerance purportedly provided by relativism. *Cf.* BERNARD WILLIAMS, MORALITY: AN INTRODUCTION TO ETHICS 14–37 (1972).
130. *See* RAWLS, LAW, *supra* note 11, at 37, 65, 80–81.
131. *See id.* at 80–81.
132. *See* RAWLS, THEORY, *supra* note 5, at 331.
133. *See* Martin S. Flaherty, *Rights, Reality, and Utopia*, 72 FORDHAM L. REV. 1789 (2004).

## Chapter 4

1. Rawls's list isn't, apparently, intended as exhaustive but rather as illustrative; *see* JOHN RAWLS, THE LAW OF PEOPLES, WITH THE IDEA OF PUBLIC REASON REVISITED 78–79 (1999) ("such as"). And even if the list *were* fixed, the interpretation of the various guarantees could obviously be contested.
2. *See* RAWLS, LAW, *supra* note 1, at 65, 78–80.
3. Univ. Dec. Hum. Rights, art. 20.
4. *Id.* art. 17.
5. *Id.* art. 18.
6. *Id.* art. 19.

7. Perhaps—*see* RAWLS, LAW, *supra* note 1, at 68—Rawls could argue that the quality of being essential to a system of social cooperation is what makes a given guarantee a *human right*, but it is unclear how this criterion would work in practice. Read as a strong claim about the voluntariness of schemes of social interaction, it would impose more limits on decent nonliberal institutions than Rawls wishes to suggest are legitimate. Read loosely, it would require very little in the way of restraint on state power. Rawls provides no guidance for the use of this criterion. *See id.*
8. *Cf.* SIMON CANEY, JUSTICE BEYOND BORDERS: A GLOBAL POLITICAL THEORY 81 (2005).
9. Rawls says this explicitly with respect to liberal peoples and comprehensive doctrines and says nothing to imply that the same would not be true for decent nonliberal peoples in the original position. RAWLS, LAW, *supra* note 1, at 34. That individual deliberators behind the veil of ignorance would be unaware which national human rights norms were *theirs* seems to flow naturally from Rawls's conception of the function of the veil of ignorance and the original position.
10. This does not mean that human rights protections will not be afforded at all. The level of human rights protection afforded in a given society will not be determined solely by the ideology dominant in that society. Each society has an interest in its own stability, and significant human rights abuses can lead to instability. The dominant actors in each society have some reason to foster the protection of human rights simply as a means of promoting stability, even if respect for some of the rights might not be required by—or might even be inconsistent with—the ideology dominant in the society. I owe this point to Seana Shiffrin.
11. Samuel Freeman, *The Law of Peoples, Social Cooperation, Human Rights, and Distributive Justice, in* JUSTICE AND GLOBAL POLITICS 29, 38 (Ellen Frankel Paul, Fred D. Miller Jr. & Jeffrey Paul eds., 2006).
12. *Cf.* RAWLS, LAW, *supra* note 1. at 80; JOHN RAWLS, *The Law of Peoples, in* COLLECTED PAPERS 529, 554–55 (Samuel Freeman ed., 1999).
13. *See* RAWLS, LAW, *supra* note 1, at 25–27.

14. *See, e.g.*, James W. Nickel, *Are Human Rights Mainly Implemented by Intervention?*, *in* RAWLS'S LAW OF PEOPLES: A REALISTIC UTOPIA? at 263 (Rex Martin & David A. Reidy eds., 2006).
15. *Cf.* David Luban, *A Theory of Crimes against Humanity*, 29 YALE J. INT'L L. 85 (2004).
16. RAWLS, LAW, *supra* note 1, at 82 (footnotes omitted).
17. JOHN RAWLS, A THEORY OF JUSTICE 53 (rev. ed., 1999). *Cf.* JOHN RAWLS, POLITICAL LIBERALISM 291–99 (1996); JOHN RAWLS, JUSTICE AS FAIRNESS: A RESTATEMENT 112–14 (Erin Kelly ed., 2000).
18. RAWLS, RESTATEMENT, *supra* note 17, at 112–13. Rawls retreated under pressure from H. L. A. Hart, *see id.* at 112. His later formulation appears to be compatible with a relatively cramped conception of personal freedom. Thus, for instance, the narrowed conception of the basic liberties in Rawls's later work means that "[s]ome kinds of speech are not specially protected." *Id.* at 113.
19. *Id.* at 114.
20. *See id.* at 158–62.
21. *See* JOHN TOMASI, FREE MARKET FAIRNESS 76–78 (2012).
22. *See id.* at 78–79.
23. *Cf. id.* at 79.
24. *See id.* at 79–81.
25. *See id.* at 82–84.
26. There is also a plausible case to be made that globally (but also, surely, domestically) specific "prohibitions on theft and fraud, provisions for enforcing contracts," and other protections for voluntary exchange might be embraced in an original position not unlike Rawls's; *see* Leif Wenar, *Contractualism and Global Economic Justice*, *in* GLOBAL JUSTICE 76, 89 (Thomas W. Pogge ed., 2001). Wenar's focus is on a global original position in which people are represented as consumers, producers, and owners, and he envisions a range of other, more specific, economic regulations that might also be endorsed. It is plausible to think that a number of the constraints Wenar contemplates might be embraced as natural duties in a Rawlsian original position; even though people in such an original position would surely think of themselves in more than narrowly economic terms, they would recognize the centrality of economic interactions

to the achievement of their other goals and might well proceed accordingly.
27. See Tomasi, *supra* note 21, at 84.
28. *See id.* at 184–91.
29. *See id.* at 228–37.
30. *See id.* at 110.
31. *Cf.* Jay R. Mandle, Globalization and the Poor (2003).
32. *But cf.* Rawls, Law, *supra* note 1, at 39, 115–19 (defending immigration restrictions).
33. *See* Gillian Brock, Global Justice: A Cosmopolitan Account 190–94 (2009).
34. *Cf.* Howard F. Chang, *The Economics of International Labor Migration and the Case for Global Distributive Justice in Liberal Political Theory*, 41 Cornell Int'l L.J. 1, 20–24 (2008) (responding to Rawlsian and related worries about open immigration policies); Fernando R. Tesón, *Brain Drain*, 45 San Diego L. Rev. 899 (2008); Michelle A. McKinley, *Conviviality, Cosmopolitan Citizenship, and Hospitality*, 5 Unbound 55, 64–68 (2009).
35. *See* John M. Finnis, *Reason, Revelation, Universality, and Particularity in Ethics*, 53 Am. J. Juris. 23, 42–45 (2008).
36. Richard W. Miller, *The Interests of the Governed and the Interests of Humanity: The Moral Importance of Borders*, 90 B.U.L. Rev. 1785, 1801 n.35 (2010).
37. Rawls, Restatement, *supra* note 17, at 44.
38. *Id.* at 112.
39. *See* John Rawls, *The Sense of Justice, in* Collected Papers, *supra* note 12, at 96, 98; *idem, Distributive Justice, in id.* at 130, 133; *idem, Justice as Fairness, in id.* at 47, 48.
40. Rawls, Theory, *supra* note 17, at 266 (my italics).
41. *See* H. L. A. Hart, *Rawls on Liberty and Its Priority*, 40 U. Chi. L.R. 534 (1973).
42. Herbert Spencer, Social Statics 78 (1851). While the similarity with Rawls's initial versions of his first principle is noteworthy, Spencer's name does not appear in the index to *A Theory of Justice*. Hart notes the obvious similarity between Rawls's and Spencer's formulations; *see* Hart, *supra* note 41, at 534.
43. *See, e.g.*, Rawls, Theory, *supra* note 17, at 131–32.

44. Rawls speaks explicitly only of the retention, not of the use, of nuclear weapons. I assume throughout, however, that he regards the use of such weapons against outlaw states as at least potentially appropriate.
45. Rawls's account of just war doctrine depends on MICHAEL WALZER, JUST AND UNJUST WARS (1977); *see* RAWLS, LAW, *supra* note 1, at 95 n.8. For an earlier version of Rawls's understanding of just war norms, minus the "supreme emergency" exception to which I object in the text, see RAWLS, THEORY, *supra* note 17, at 332–35.
46. RAWLS, LAW, *supra* note 1, at 96.
47. *See id.* at 95–97.
48. *See id.* at 95; *cf.* Rawls's developed account: JOHN RAWLS, *Fifty Years after Hiroshima*, in COLLECTED PAPERS, *supra* note 12, at 565.
49. RAWLS, LAW, *supra* note 1, at 101. Rawls's characterization of Churchill's remarks makes me confident that Rawls shares Churchill's retrospective assessment; *see id.* at 100.
50. As Rawls notes, this expression comes from Michael Walzer: *see* WALZER, *supra* note 45, at 255–65.
51. *See* RAWLS, LAW, *supra* note 1, at 98.
52. *See id.* at 9.
53. *Id.* at 99.
54. *Contra* Leif Wenar, *Why Rawls Is Not a Cosmopolitan Liberal*, in RAWLS'S LAW OF PEOPLES: A REALISTIC UTOPIA? 95, 109 (Rex Martin & David A. Reidy eds., 2006); *cf. id.* at 113 n.42. Wenar apparently expects the reader to regard the US government's invasion of Iraq as obviously appropriate, so that a principle that ruled it out, or that precluded actions reasonably undertaken in connection with it, would seem uncontroversially mistaken.
55. Darrell Cole, *09.11.01: Death before Dishonor or Dishonor before Death: Christian Just War, Terrorism, and Supreme Emergency*, 16 NOTRE DAME J.L. ETHICS & PUB. POL'Y 81, 93–98 (2002); *cf.* David S. Koller, *The Moral Imperative: Toward a Human Rights-Based Law of War*, 46 HARV. INT'L L.J. 231 (2005).
56. *Cf.* RAWLS, THEORY, *supra* note 1, at 333.
57. Even if tactical nuclear weapons proved easier to deliver or less costly than conventional weapons, it seems clear that individual

deliberators would not regard these considerations as at least ordinarily justifying their use, given the risks their employment could pose to noncombatants. *Cf.* Lionel K. McPherson, *Excessive Force in War: A "Golden Rule" Test*, 7 THEORETICAL INQ. L. 81 (2006).
58. *See* RAWLS, LAW, *supra* note 1, at 9. Rawls refers specifically to nuclear weapons in the cited passage.
59. Cole, *supra* note 55, at 90.
60. RAWLS, LAW, *supra* note 1, at 98.
61. *Id.* at 99.
62. *See id.* at 98.
63. *See* JOHN M. FINNIS, JOSEPH M. BOYLE JR. & GERMAIN G. GRISEZ, NUCLEAR DETERRENCE, MORALITY, AND REALISM (1987).
64. *See* RAWLS, LAW, *supra* note 1, at 105.
65. *See id.*
66. *See id.* at 105.
67. *See id.* at 104.
68. *Id.* at 105 (emphasis added). Rawls also maintains that someone who "oppose[s] all war" cannot "in good faith, in the absence of special circumstances, seek the highest offices in a liberal democratic regime." *Id.* If so, this may simply be evidence of the moral bankruptcy of liberal democratic regimes. But is it so obvious that a liberal regime must be prepared, if necessary, to go to war under some circumstances? No doubt political liberalism on its own is compatible with a variety of answers to this question, but it cannot, I think, be reasonably understood as imposing a *duty* on a politician in a liberal people to opt for war, even assuming the acceptability of the state. *Cf.* STANLEY HAUERWAS, AGAINST THE NATIONS: WAR AND SURVIVAL IN A LIBERAL SOCIETY (1985).
69. *See* RAWLS, LAW, *supra* note 1.
70. *Cf.* Cole, *supra* note 55, at 92 (noting that the proponent of traditional just war norms "argues that it is better to be occupied by a people such as the Nazis than to behave like Nazis").
71. *See, e.g.*, GARY CHARTIER, THE CONSCIENCE OF AN ANARCHIST 53–68 (2011); RUDOLPH JOSEPH RUMMEL, STATISTICS OF DEMOCIDE: GENOCIDE AND MASS MURDER SINCE 1900 (1997); [Matthew White,] *Source List and Detailed Death Tolls for the Twentieth Century Hemoclysm*, HISTORICAL ATLAS OF

THE TWENTIETH CENTURY, http://www.erols.com/mwhite28/warstat1.htm.
72. *Cf.* ANDREW KUPER, DEMOCRACY BEYOND BORDERS: JUSTICE AND REPRESENTATION IN GLOBAL INSTITUTIONS 18–24 (2004).
73. *See* RAWLS, LAW, *supra* note 1, at 62.
74. *Id.* at 62.
75. *Id.* at 83.
76. *Id.*
77. *See id.* at 60.
78. *See id.* at 84–85.
79. *See id.* at 61.
80. Alec Walen, *The Significance of Rawls's Law of Peoples*, 6 INT'L LEGAL THEORY 51, 53 (2000).
81. *Cf.* KOK-CHOR TAN, TOLERATION, DIVERSITY, AND GLOBAL JUSTICE 35 (2000).
82. Such associations can, of course, impose nonviolent sanctions that are exceptionally costly from the standpoints of their members; consider, for example, a religious community that claims the right to determine its members' ultimate destinies. *Cf.* BRIAN BARRY, CULTURE AND EQUALITY: AN EGALITARIAN CRITIQUE OF MULTICULTURALISM (2001).
83. Thanks to Seana Shiffrin for helping me to see the need to stress this point. *Cf.* RAWLS, RESTATEMENT, *supra* note 17, at 93–94; RAWLS, LIBERALISM, *supra* note 17, at 136 n.4.
84. *See* RAWLS, LAW, *supra* note 1, at 84–85. I ignore in the text Rawls's treatment of the International Monetary Fund (IMF) or its equivalent in his imagined Society of Peoples. He notes that the IMF often does attach conditions to loans that have the effect of promoting what he takes to be the development of liberal institutions, but I suspect even the IMF's practice can be made consistent with his general point on the thesis that its putative goal is not to promote liberalization *per se* but rather to foster political conditions that seem to conduce to loan repayment, an economic objective that any country supporting the Fund would have reason to share. *See id.* at 85 n.30. In any event, not all countries belong to the IMF, and there might be less ideological conflict of the sort to which Rawls alludes within a less inclusive organization.

85. *Cf.* Thomas W. Pogge, *Rawls on International Justice*, 51 PHIL. Q. 246, 248 (2001).
86. RAWLS, LAW, *supra* note 1, at 85.
87. *See id.*
88. *See id.* at 84–85.
89. *See, e.g.*, CHRIS COYNE, DOING BAD BY DOING GOOD: WHY HUMANITARIAN ACTION FAILS (2013); DAMBISA MOYO, DEAD AID: WHY AID IS NOT WORKING AND HOW THERE IS A BETTER WAY FOR AFRICA (2010); R. GLENN HUBBARD & WILLIAM DUGGAN, THE AID TRAP: HARD TRUTHS ABOUT ENDING POVERTY (2009). *Cf.* DAVID SCHMIDTZ, *Separateness, Suffering, and Moral Theory*, *in* PERSON, POLIS, PLANET: ESSAYS IN APPLIED PHILOSOPHY 145 (2008); Neera K. Badhwar, *International Aid: When Giving Becomes a Vice*, *in* JUSTICE AND GLOBAL POLITICS 69 (Ellen Frankel Paul, Fred D. Miller Jr. & Jeffrey Paul eds., 2006).
90. While Rawls is clearly committed to gender justice on practical and moral grounds—*see* RAWLS, LAW, *supra* note 1, at 110—the kind of consultation procedure he imagines would not ensure the equality of women and so might not secure their human rights very reliably.
91. *Id.* at 85.
92. This is likely to be particularly true with respect to the interests of women; *cf.* Catherine Powell, *Lifting Our Veil of Ignorance: Culture, Constitutionalism, and Women's Human Rights in Post-September 11 America*, 57 HASTINGS L.J. 331 (2005).
93. Which is not to say that this is an option Rawls would necessarily endorse; *see, e.g.*, A. John Simmons, *Disobedience and Its Objects*, 90 B.U.L. REV. 1805, 1827 n.103 (2010).
94. JON MANDLE, GLOBAL JUSTICE 83 (2006).
95. *Cf.* CANEY, *supra* note 8, at 80 (noting that one could accept "the slogan 'cosmopolitanism for persons and Rawlsianism for peoples'").
96. For a critique of Rawls's notion of toleration, *see id.* at 48–51.
97. Of course, nonliberals might offer incentives to liberals to encourage them to adopt *their* ways of life; *see* Mortimer Sellers, *The Law of Peoples*, 6 INT'L LEGAL THEORY 44, 48–49 (2000).

## Chapter 5

1. *See* JOHN TOMASI, FREE MARKET FAIRNESS (2012).
2. Tomasi borrows this expression, which he employs ironically, from Samuel Freeman.
3. At least one critic has already referred to Tomasi's approach as an instance of "right-wing Rawlsianism." People are doubtless free to use terms however they like, and the sort of position I have sought to defend here and elsewhere is certainly more radical and more leftist than Tomasi's; *see, e.g.*, MARKETS NOT CAPITALISM: INDIVIDUALIST ANARCHISM AGAINST BOSSES, INEQUALITY, CORPORATE POWER, AND STRUCTURAL POVERTY (Gary Chartier & Charles W. Johnson eds., 2011). But it is difficult for me to see why a propeace, pro-civil-liberties position that is sincerely motivated by concern for the least well off and that realistically grounds and expresses that concern should be seen as "right wing" in the pejorative sense in which that expression is frequently (and often quite reasonably) used. Tomasi may, of course, be wrong; but he is neither morally obtuse nor an authoritarian, a proponent of hierarchy, a racist, a nationalist, a militarist, a corporate apologist, or anything comparable.
4. This presumption has been questioned by, *e.g.*, JAMES FISHKIN, TYRANNY AND LEGITIMACY: A CRITIQUE OF POLITICAL THEORIES 105–20 (1979).
5. *See* JOHN RAWLS, THE LAW OF PEOPLES, WITH THE IDEA OF PUBLIC REASON REVISITED 120 (1999).
6. *See id.* at 117.
7. *See* DAVID C. ROSE, MORAL FOUNDATIONS OF ECONOMIC BEHAVIOR (2011).
8. *Cf.* Thomas W. Pogge, *Rawls on International Justice*, 51 PHIL. Q. 246, 251–53 (2001).
9. *See* Charles Beitz, *Rawls's Law of Peoples*, 110 ETHICS 669, 690 (2000); Allen Buchanan, *Rawls's Law of Peoples: Rules for a Vanished Westphalian World*, 110 ETHICS 697, 705–9 (2000); ALLEN BUCHANAN, JUSTICE, LEGITIMACY, AND SELF-DETERMINATION: MORAL FOUNDATIONS FOR INTERNATIONAL LAW 212–15 (2004).
10. *See* Samuel Freeman, *Distributive Justice and the Law of Peoples*, *in* RAWLS'S LAW OF PEOPLES: A REALISTIC UTOPIA? 243 (Rex Martin & David A. Reidy eds., 2006); Samuel Freeman, *The*

*Law of Peoples, Social Cooperation, Human Rights, and Distributive Justice, in* JUSTICE AND GLOBAL POLITICS 29 (Ellen Frankel Paul, Fred D. Miller Jr. & Jeffrey Paul eds., 2006).

11. Edward Foley argues that deliberators at the global level would not embrace a version of the Difference Principle; *see* Edward Foley, *Human Rights Theory: The Elusive Quest for Global Justice*, 66 FORDHAM L. REV. 249, 258–65 (1997). But Foley supposes that a powerful global state would be needed to implement the Principle, which would not be true on the version I endorse here. *Cf.* Frank J. Garcia, *Building a Just Trade Order for a New Millennium*, 33 GEO. WASH. INT'L L. REV. 1015 (2001); *idem*, *Trade and Inequality: Economic Justice and the Developing World*, 21 MICH. J. INT'L L. 975, 1015–18 (2000). Individual deliberators at the global level who didn't embrace the Difference Principle might also, of course, opt for a variety of related or similar but nonetheless distinct principles more demanding than the one Rawls endorses; *see* Allen Buchanan, *Rawls's Law of Peoples: Rules for a Vanished Westphalian World*, 110 ETHICS 697, 711 (2000).

12. Though the Difference Principle is not, as Rawls emphasizes, a principle of rectification, implementing a principle of rectification could contribute significantly to affecting the background conditions in ways beneficial to the global poor.

13. *See, e.g.*, CHRIS COYNE, DOING BAD BY DOING GOOD: WHY HUMANITARIAN ACTION FAILS (2013); DAMBISA MOYO, DEAD AID: WHY AID IS NOT WORKING AND HOW THERE IS A BETTER WAY FOR AFRICA (2010); R. GLENN HUBBARD & WILLIAM DUGGAN, THE AID TRAP: HARD TRUTHS ABOUT ENDING POVERTY (2009). *Cf.* DAVID SCHMIDTZ, *Separateness, Suffering, and Moral Theory, in* PERSON, POLIS, PLANET: ESSAYS IN APPLIED PHILOSOPHY 145 (2008); Neera K. Badhwar, *International Aid: When Giving Becomes a Vice, in* JUSTICE AND GLOBAL POLITICS, *supra* note 10, at 69.

14. *See, e.g.*, LIAM B. MURPHY, MORAL DEMANDS IN NONIDEAL THEORY (2003); MARTHA NUSSBAUM, FRONTIERS OF JUSTICE: DISABILITY, NATIONALITY, SPECIES MEMBERSHIP 224–324 (2006); HENRY SHUE, BASIC RIGHTS: SUBSISTENCE, AFFLUENCE, AND US FOREIGN POLICY (2d ed. 1996); Thomas Nagel, *The Problem of Global Justice*, 33 PHIL. & PUB. AFFAIRS 113 (2005);

STANLEY HOFFMAN, DUTIES BEYOND BORDERS: ON THE LIMITS AND POSSIBILITIES OF ETHICAL INTERNATIONAL POLITICS (1981); Thomas Nagel, *Poverty and Food: Why Charity Is Not Enough*, in FOOD POLICY: THE RESPONSIBILITY OF THE UNITED STATES IN THE LIFE AND DEATH CHOICES (Peter Brown & Henry Shue eds., 1977); T. M. SCANLON, WHAT WE OWE TO EACH OTHER 224 (1998); ONORA O'NEILL, TOWARDS JUSTICE AND VIRTUE: A CONSTRUCTIVE ACCOUNT OF PRACTICAL REASON 196–200 (1996); ONORA O'NEILL, FACES OF HUNGER: AN ESSAY ON POVERTY, JUSTICE, AND DEVELOPMENT (1986). *Cf.* Lea Brilmayer, *International Justice and International Law*, 98 W. VA. L. REV. 611 (1996).
15. TOMASI, *supra* note 1, at 285 n.86.
16. *Cf.* Roderick T. Long, *Liberty: The Other Equality*, THE FREEMAN: IDEAS ON LIBERTY, Oct. 2005, at 17, http://www.fee.org/pdf/the-freeman/0510Long.pdf; Roderick T. Long, *Equality: The Unknown Ideal*, MISES DAILY, Oct. 16, 2001, http:www.mises.org/story/804.
17. TOMASI, *supra* note 1, at 88.
18. *Id.*
19. *Cf.* CHANDRAN KUKATHAS, THE LIBERAL ARCHIPELAGO: A THEORY OF DIVERSITY AND FREEDOM 85 (2003).
20. *See, e.g.*, ANARCHY, STATE, AND PUBLIC CHOICE (Edward P. Stringham ed., 2005); ANTHONY DE JASAY, THE STATE (1998); MICHAEL TAYLOR, COMMUNITY, ANARCHY, AND LIBERTY (1982); MICHAEL TAYLOR, THE POSSIBILITY OF COOPERATION (1987).
21. *See, e.g.*, HEDLEY BULL, THE ANARCHICAL SOCIETY: A STUDY OF ORDER IN WORLD POLITICS (1977); Alexander Wendt, *Anarchy Is What States Make of It: The Social Construction of Power Politics*, 46 INT'L ORG. 391 (1992).
22. *See* Roderick T. Long, *Market Anarchism as Constitutionalism*, in ANARCHISM/MINARCHISM: IS A GOVERNMENT PART OF A FREE COUNTRY? 133 (Roderick T. Long & Tibor Machan eds., 2008).
23. *Cf.* ANDREW KUPER, DEMOCRACY BEYOND BORDERS: JUSTICE AND REPRESENTATION IN GLOBAL INSTITUTIONS 30 (2004).
24. *See generally id.*
25. *Id.* at 32.

26. *Id.* at 197.
27. *See id.* at 5.
28. *See, e.g., id.* at 158–78.
29. *See, e.g., id.* at 33.
30. *See, e.g.,* Tom W. Bell, *Polycentric Law in a New Century,* Policy, Aut. 1999, at 34; John Hasnas, *The Depoliticization of Law,* 9 Theoretical Inquiries in Law 529 (2008).
31. *See* Michael Huemer, The Problem of Political Authority: An Examination of the Right to Coerce and the Duty to Obey 86–93, 171–72 (2013). Huemer develops a considerably more elaborate account of fair play arguments than I seek to do here; I believe his account deserves to be nuanced in at least two ways: (*i*) He suggests that the issue of fair play arises when "a large good" is at stake, *id.* at 87, but it seems to me that one might think that this was true, at least often, only when the good was not so much substantial as, rather, essential for the achievement of other goods. The provision by some of inessential goods in great quantities might not seem to obligate others to assist. (*ii*) He denies that willingly taking advantage of the goods produced is necessary for a fair play argument to get off the ground, but while this might be true in some emergency situations (as in the lifeboat example he employs), this doesn't show that willing participation isn't ordinarily required.
32. *See id.* at 89–90.
33. *See, e.g.,* Gary Chartier, Anarchy and Legal Order: Law and Politics for a Stateless Society (2013).
34. *See* Tomasi, *supra* note 1, at 199–200.
35. *See, e.g.,* Kevin A. Carson, *Another Free-for-All: Libertarian Class Analysis, Organized Labor, Etc.*, Mutualist Blog: Free Market Anti-Capitalism, Jan. 26, 2006, http://mutualist .blogspot.com/2006/01/another-free-for-all-libertarian-class .html; Wally Conger, Agorist Class Theory: A Left Libertarian Approach to Class Conflict Analysis (n.d.), http:// www.agorism.info/AgoristClassTheory.pdf; Walter E. Grinder and John Hagel, *Toward a Theory of State Capitalism: Ultimate Decision Making and Class Structure,* 1 J. Libertarian Stud. 59 (1977); David M. Hart, The Radical Liberalism of Charles Comte and Charles Dunoyer (1994) (unpublished PhD dissertation, University of Cambridge); Hans-Hermann Hoppe,

*Marxist and Austrian Class Analysis*, 9 J. LIBERTARIAN STUD. 79 (1990); Roderick T. Long, *Toward a Libertarian Theory of Class*, 15 SOC. PHIL. & POL'Y 303 (1998); ALBERT JAY NOCK, OUR ENEMY THE STATE (1935); CARL OGLESBY, THE YANKEE AND COWBOY WAR (1977); FRANZ OPPENHEIMER, THE STATE (1997); TOM G. PALMER, *Classical Liberalism, Marxism, and the Conflict of Classes: The Classical Liberal Theory of Class Conflict, in* REALIZING FREEDOM: LIBERTARIAN THEORY, HISTORY, AND PRACTICE 255–76 (2009); Sheldon Richman, *Class Struggle Rightly Conceived*, THE FREEMAN: IDEAS ON LIBERTY, July 13, 2007, http://www.thefreemanonline.org/columns/tgif/class-struggle-rightly-conceived. *Cf.* C. WRIGHT MILLS, THE POWER ELITE (1956); G. WILLIAM DOMHOFF, WHO RULES AMERICA? CHALLENGES TO CORPORATE AND CLASS DOMINANCE (6th ed., 2009).
36. *Cf.* Jeremy Weiland, *Let the Free Market Eat the Rich, in* MARKETS NOT CAPITALISM, *supra* note 3, at 301, *available at* http://anarchywithoutbombs.com/2010/03/13/let-the-free-market-eat-the-rich.
37. *See, e.g.*, JOHN RAWLS, JUSTICE AS FAIRNESS: A RESTATEMENT 130–31 (Erin Kelly ed., 2000).
38. *Cf.* Charles W. Johnson, *Scratching By: How Government Creates Poverty as We Know It, in* MARKETS NOT CAPITALISM, *supra* note 3, at 377, *available at* http://www.thefreemanonline.org/featured/scratching-by-how-government-creates-poverty-as-we-know-it.
39. *See, e.g.*, Jason Brennan, *Rawls's Paradox*, 18 CONST. POL. ECON. 287 (2007); DAVID SCHMIDTZ, *Guarantees, in* PERSON, POLIS, PLANET: ESSAYS IN APPLIED PHILOSOPHY 174 (2008).
40. I cannot emphasize strongly enough that this implies no inclination whatsoever "to defend, willy nilly, all property which now is called private." This is because "[m]uch of that property is stolen. Much is of dubious title. All of it is deeply intertwined with an immoral, coercive state system which has condoned, built on, and profited from slavery; has expanded through and exploited a brutal and aggressive imperial and colonial foreign policy, and continues to hold the people in a roughly serf-master relationship to political-economic power concentrations." Karl Hess, *Letter from Washington: What Are the Specifics?*, LIBERTARIAN FORUM, June 15, 1969, at 2.

41. *See* JOHN RAWLS, A THEORY OF JUSTICE 93–95 (rev. ed., 1999).
42. *Id.* at 93.
43. *Id.* at 95.
44. Wilfried Hinsch acknowledges that institutions as such, including peoples, cannot have natural duties. But he maintains that peoples can have duties analogous to the natural duties of particular persons. *See* Wilfried Hinsch, *Global Distributive Justice*, *in* GLOBAL JUSTICE 55, 62–63 (Thomas W. Pogge ed., 2001). I think the notion that organizations have moral responsibilities (and rights) distinguishable from those of their members is problematic; I believe it would be simpler to observe, in light of the fact that persons have natural duties, (*i*) that the institutions in which persons participate (voluntarily and cooperatively) can provide mechanisms through which they can fulfill these duties and (*ii*) that the operation of these institutions affects the context of individual persons' actions (as by creating live possibilities of coordination; *see* Leif Wenar, *Contractualism and Global Economic Justice*, *in* GLOBAL JUSTICE, *supra*, at 76, 79 n.2) and thus, in at least some cases, the specific contents of their natural duties.
45. *See* DAVID SCHMIDTZ, ELEMENTS OF JUSTICE 90–93 (2006).

## Conclusion

1. JOHN RAWLS, THE LAW OF PEOPLES, WITH THE IDEA OF PUBLIC REASON REVISITED 17 n.9 (1999).
2. *Cf.* Lea Brilmayer, *What Use Is John Rawls' Theory of Justice to Public International Law?*, 6 INT'L LEGAL THEORY 36, 37 (2000); Todd Adams, *Using Justice as Fairness in Reducing Global Greenhouse Emissions*, 16 J. ENVTL. L. & LITIG. 331, 371–72 (2001).
3. *But cf.* JOHN RAWLS, *The Law of Peoples*, *in* COLLECTED PAPERS 529, 549 (Samuel Freeman ed., 1999) (suggesting that individual and Rawlsian deliberators might be expected to reach the same conclusions).
4. RAWLS, LAW, *supra* note 1, at 120 (emphasis added).
5. *See id.*
6. *See* RAWLS, LAW, *supra* note 1, at 62; *cf.* JOHN RAWLS, POLITICAL LIBERALISM 62 (1996).

# About the Author

GARY CHARTIER is Professor of Law and Business Ethics and Associate Dean of the Tom and Vi Zapara School of Business at La Sierra University in Riverside, California. He is the author of *Anarchy and Legal Order* (Cambridge, 2013), *Economic Justice and Natural Law* (Cambridge, 2009), *The Conscience of an Anarchist* (Cobden, 2011), and *The Analogy of Love* (Imprint Academic, 2007) as well as the coeditor (with Charles W. Johnson) of *Markets Not Capitalism: Individualist Anarchism against Bosses, Inequality, Corporate Power, and Structural Poverty* (Minor Compositions-Autonomedia, 2011) and (with Ross Kenyon and Roderick T. Long) *Libertarian Theories of Class* (forthcoming). His byline has appeared nearly forty times in journals including the *Oxford Journal of Legal Studies*, *Legal Theory*, *Law and Philosophy*, and the *UCLA Law Review*. He is a member of the American Philosophical Association and the Alliance of the Libertarian Left and a senior fellow of the Center for a Stateless Society.

After receiving a BA in history and political science from La Sierra (1987, *magna cum laude*), he explored ethics, theology, Christian origins, the philosophy of religion, and political philosophy at the University of Cambridge, earning a PhD (1991) with a dissertation on the idea of friendship. He graduated with a JD (2001, Order of the Coif) from UCLA, where he studied legal philosophy and constitutional law and earned the Judge Jerry Pacht Memorial Award in Constitutional Law. Visit him online at http://www.garychartier.net.

# Index

Adams, Todd, 187
AntiWar.com, x
association, freedom of, 109, 110
Austrian School, 186

Badhwar, Neera, 181, 183
Barry, Brian, 180
Beitz, Charles, ix, 159, 163, 164, 182
Bell, Tom W., 185
Boyle, Joseph M., Jr., 179
Brennan, Jason, 186
Brilmayer, Lea, 162, 165, 166, 184, 187
Brock, Gillian, 92, 159, 177
Buchanan, Allen, 160, 165, 167, 182, 183

calculation, economic, 91
Caney, Simon, 160, 162, 175, 181
capitalism, 157, 182, 185, 186, 189
Carson, Kevin A., x, 185
Churchill, Winston, 178
class analysis, 140, 141
codes, building, 141
Cole, Darrell, 178, 179
communitarianism, 73
competition, 33, 42, 147

Comte, Charles, 185
corporation, 126, 132, 138, 182
Coyne, Christopher, 181, 183
criminal law, 56, 106

doctrine, comprehensive, 9, 10, 41, 42, 43, 44, 45, 46, 47, 48, 49, 50, 52, 53, 54, 59, 63, 77, 106, 139, 170, 175
Domhoff, G. William, 186
Dunoyer, Charles, 185

education, 24, 164
elections, voting, 87, 134
empire, imperialism, x, 58, 108, 186
entrepreneurship, 127, 128, 132
equality, inequality, 7, 8, 13, 14, 15, 16, 17, 18, 20, 23, 25, 26, 27, 28, 29, 45, 47, 49, 50, 51, 52, 53, 55, 57, 66, 73, 74, 75, 76, 77, 78, 79, 82, 92, 106, 110, 114, 134, 137, 151, 152, 153, 156, 161, 166, 170, 173, 181
exit, costs of, 59, 110, 111, 112

Finnis, John M., ix, 93, 164, 172, 177, 179
Fishkin, James, 182

Franck, Thomas M., 167
Freeman, Samuel, 84, 125, 158, 162, 169, 172, 175, 182, 187
friendship, ix, x, 93, 189

gender, gender relations, 82, 110, 111, 181
Germany, 102
Gillis, William, x
Gordon, David, ix, x, 163, 168, 170, 172
Gregory, Anthony, x
Grinder, Walter E., 185
Grisez, Germain, 179

Hagel, John, 185
Hart, H. L. A., 94, 95, 96, 97, 176, 177, 185
Hayden, Patrick, ix, 165, 170
Hayek, Friedrich, 157
Hess, Karl, 186
hierarchy, 9, 10, 15, 20, 91, 110, 115, 141, 182
Hinsch, Wilfried, 187
Hiroshima, 178
Holmes, Oliver Wendell, 173
homesteading, 132
Huemer, Michael, 160, 162, 185
Hume, David, iv

individuality, 10, 15, 18, 26, 29, 56, 57, 71, 99, 151, 156, 159, 187
International Monetary Fund (IMF), 180
Iraq, 178

Jasay, Anthony de, 184
Johnson, Charles W., x, 157, 182, 186, 189
justice
 as fairness, 14, 41, 42, 43, 44, 45, 47, 49, 54, 61, 67, 74, 76, 77, 78, 87, 90, 144, 161, 166, 168, 170, 176, 177, 186, 187
 social, 140

Kant, Immanuel, 170
Keaton, Angela, x
Kinzer, Craig, x
Knapp, Thomas, x
Koh, Harold, 167
Kukathas, Chandran, 170, 184
Kuper, Andrew, 121, 134, 135, 136, 148, 180, 184

labor unions, 124
land, 132, 141
land-use regulation, 141
Larmore, Charles, 162
liberalism, cosmopolitan, 27, 35, 46, 47, 49, 50, 51, 62, 86, 109, 116, 159
licenses, licensing, 88, 98, 129, 141, 152
Long, Roderick T., x, 184, 186, 189
Luban, David, 176

Machan, Tibor, 184
Mandle, Jay, 177
Mandle, Jon, 116, 181
Marx, Karl, 186
migration, 92, 93, 111, 112, 126, 127, 131, 177

Miller, Richard, 93, 165, 172, 177
monopoly, 11, 32, 65, 69, 111, 136, 140, 141, 144, 145, 146, 148, 153
mutualist, mutualism, 185

Nagel, Thomas, 172, 183, 184
nationalism, 182
Nazism, 102, 179
nuclear weapons, 98, 99, 100, 101, 105, 152, 178, 179
Nussbaum, Martha, 172, 183

O'Neill, Onora, 184
opinion and expression, freedom of, 83
Oppenheimer, Franz, 186
organizations, international, iv
ownership, 83, 151, 154

Pateman, Carole, ix, x, 160, 161
Pettit, Philip, 70, 71, 72, 73, 172
Pogge, Thomas, ix, 159, 160, 161, 164, 165, 176, 181, 182, 187
poverty, 7, 90, 92, 93, 123, 124, 125, 126, 127, 128, 129, 130, 131, 132, 139, 141, 142, 143, 146, 155, 156, 183, 186
Powell, Catherine, 181
public choice, 140

racism, 182
redistribution, 125, 128, 130, 131, 140, 141, 142, 143, 144, 167

relativism, 27, 76, 77, 78, 79, 80, 172, 173, 174
Richman, Sheldon, x, 186
Rorty, Richard M., 173
Rustad, Roger E., Jr., ix, x, 166

Scanlon, Thomas M., 165, 184
Schmidtz, David, ix, 181, 183, 186, 187
science, natural, 141, 189
secession, secessionism, 171
Sellers, Mortimer, 181
sexuality, 84, 85, 106
Shue, Henry, 183, 184
Simmons, A. John, 171
Simon, Herbert, 160, 162, 175
slavery, 67, 147, 186
socialism, 91, 118
sovereignty, iv, 6, 64, 65, 67, 68, 69, 70, 85, 121, 134, 136, 140, 155
Spangler, Brad, x
Spencer, Herbert, 94, 177
Stromberg, Joseph L., x
subsidies, 113, 114, 117, 138, 141

taxes, xi, 113, 128, 130, 131, 141
Taylor, Michael, 184
Tesón, Fernando, ix, 26, 165, 172, 177
Thomas Aquinas, 103
toleration, 10, 17, 18, 19, 25, 77, 79, 80, 81, 105, 109, 110, 111, 116, 117, 174, 181
Tomasi, John, ix, 2, 82, 87, 89, 90, 91, 92, 121, 122, 123, 124, 133, 134, 137, 140, 142, 143, 147, 148, 149,

Tomasi, John (*continued*)
  152, 154, 156, 176, 177,
  182, 184, 185
trade, free, 127, 130, 131
Tushnet, Mark, 163, 164

Waldron, Jeremy, 168
Walzer, Michael, 178
war, x, 2, 6, 8, 10, 14, 20, 38,
  39, 49, 58, 62, 64, 69, 80,
  81, 85, 86, 97, 98, 99, 100,
  101, 102, 103, 104, 105,
  107, 108, 109, 110, 115,
  116, 118, 128, 129, 130,
  139, 140, 151, 152, 154,
  156, 168, 179

justice in, 98, 99, 100, 101,
  102, 103, 105, 107, 178,
  179
Webb, Elenor, v, ix, x
Weiland, Jeremy, x, 141, 186
Wenar, Leif, 58, 59, 64, 169,
  171, 176, 178, 187
Williams, Bernard, 167, 174
workplaces, 91
world government, 2, 3, 28, 31,
  32, 33, 36, 37, 38, 40, 65,
  73, 125, 135, 155
World Trade Organization, 92,
  127

Zanetti, Véronique, 32, 165, 166